Get Started in Reiki

I dedicate the essence of this book to my sister Jane, whose courage and determination in the face of adversity are inspirational, and to Max Kay – a miracle Reiki baby.

Teach Yourself®

Get Started in Reiki

Sandi Leir-Shuffrey

For UK order enquiries: please contact Bookpoint Ltd,
130 Milton Park, Abingdon, Oxon OX14 4SB.
Telephone: +44 (0) 1235 827720. Fax: +44 (0) 1235 400454.
Lines are open 09.00–17.00, Monday to Saturday, with a 24-hour
message answering service. Details about our titles and how to
order are available at www.teachyourself.com

For USA order enquiries: please contact McGraw-Hill Customer
Services, PO Box 545, Blacklick, OH 43004-0545, USA.
Telephone: 1-800-722-4726. Fax: 1-614-755-5645.

For Canada order enquiries: please contact McGraw-Hill Ryerson
Ltd, 300 Water St, Whitby, Ontario L1N 9B6, Canada.
Telephone: 905 430 5000. Fax: 905 430 5020.

Long renowned as the authoritative source for self-guided
learning – with more than 50 million copies sold worldwide –
the *Teach Yourself* series includes over 500 titles in the fields of
languages, crafts, hobbies, business, computing and education.

British Library Cataloguing in Publication Data: a catalogue record
for this title is available from the British Library.

Library of Congress Catalog Card Number: on file.

First published in UK 2000 by Hodder Education, part of Hachette
UK, 338 Euston Road, London NW13BH.

First published in US 2000 by The McGraw-Hill Companies, Inc.

This edition published 2010.

Previously published as *Teach Yourself Reiki*.

The *Teach Yourself* name is a registered trade mark of Hodder Headline.

Copyright © 2000, 2003, 2007, 2010 Sandi Leir-Shuffrey

Typeset by Macmillan Publishing Solutions.

Printed in Great Britain for Hodder Education, an Hachette UK
Company, 338 Euston Road, London NW1 3BH, by CPI Cox &
Wyman, Reading, Berkshire RG1 8EX.

The publisher has used its best endeavours to ensure that the URLs for
external websites referred to in this book are correct and active at the
time of going to press. However, the publisher and the author have
no responsibility for the websites and can make no guarantee that a
site will remain live or that the content will remain relevant, decent or
appropriate.

Hachette UK's policy is to use papers that are natural, renewable
and recyclable products and made from wood grown in sustainable
forests. The logging and manufacturing processes are expected to
conform to the environmental regulations of the country of origin.

The author and publisher take no responsibility for accident,
injury or any other consequence of following the exercises herein.
Students practise at their own risk.

Impression number   10 9 8 7 6 5 4 3 2 1

Year   2014 2013 2012 2011 2010

Acknowledgements

I acknowledge my dearest children Kim and Taz and all those students who have been inspired enough by these words to practise and find peace. I acknowledge my soul sisters and partners in crime, without whom life would not be as bright: Emma Foss-Sims, Penny Prince, Carolyn Finlay, Sue Kay, Andrea Rose, and also Rory Block who sings it like it is.

I sincerely thank the team at Hodder for the opportunity to keep reaching to empower people through the whole *Teach Yourself* series.

Permission is acknowledged for the photographs of Masters from Phyllis Furamoto.

Sandi Leir-Shuffrey

Contents

Meet the author

Welcome to *Get Started in Reiki*!

It is more than 20 years since I was fortunate enough to cross paths with Reiki. I knew instantly that it was something I would benefit from but had no idea it would be such an essential part of my daily life. There were no Reiki classes back in 1988, so I organized one and have been doing so ever since. Soon after beginning to practise on myself, I began to feel a change take place, more in my attitude, spirit and inner strength than in anything physical. I found myself feeling less out of control and more assertive; I could at last stand up for myself and believe in my own opinions. I felt that the only thing holding me back from achieving happiness was my own limitations.

Reiki boosted my confidence, as it required so little of my effort yet made such a great change. Wonderful new opportunities and people began to appear. In 1989 I was privileged to be asked to train as a full teaching Reiki Master, which I accepted without hesitation. I moved to the Gloucestershire countryside and set up the Stillpoint School of Reiki to offer both treatment and training. People travel to Stillpoint from all over the United Kingdom, Europe and even occasionally from America and the Middle East.

Every day I give thanks for the opportunity to lead other people to the gift and experience of Reiki practice. Seeing the changes in people's faces in just two days proves I have the greatest job in the world.

Only got a minute?

We have all experienced stress in our lives. In order to be happy and healthy we need to have a quiet mind, calm emotions and a relaxed body. We need time in solitude in which to reflect and restore our vitality.

'Reiki' is the Japanese word for 'universal life force'. It is the energy within and around us. The 'Usui Shiki Ryoho', the original Western form of Reiki is a simple, practical technique for hands-on healing that can be easily learnt by anyone and used in everyday life.

After a short course it is possible to apply Reiki in a full body treatment to family members, friends, pets and even as a personal self-treatment. Further instruction can activate deeper mental and emotional healing that brings about spiritual change and self-mastery.

Anyone can learn this simple technique for the purpose of healing, on all levels. When used in a focused, meditative way, Reiki can also be a direct pathway to spiritual enlightenment.

5 Only got five minutes?

The art of healing is nothing new. Every parent has the instinct to reach out to their crying child and soothe it with their hands, seeking out the discomfort with stroking, holding, touching, loving and closeness. Many forms of healing have evolved, from early systems using herbs, ritual, invocation and retreat, to the highly intelligent, holistic systems created by people such as the ancient Indian Rishis (The Vedas), the Essenes (The Dead Sea Scrolls), the Egyptians (Nay Hammadi Texts), Native American Shamans (oral tradition), Early Greeks (mythology), Christians (the Bible), Muslims (the Qur'an).

Most holistic healing systems rely on several things:

▶ *the willingness of the receiver/student to receive*
▶ *the presence of a system of knowledge to reconnect the receiver to the quantum field, or Universal Spirit, that is to say, knowledge of God through practice of the form*
▶ *the balance of Chi*
▶ *the experience and compassion of the healer to step aside, allowing self-empowerment through self-referral, self-knowledge and trust*
▶ *the shift of focus from Self to Source*
▶ *Divine Grace.*

It is believed that the early form of Reiki was used by Buddhist monks – there is evidence dating back to 206 BC – although its usage faded over the centuries. Our present-day form was rediscovered in the late-nineteenth century by a Buddhist monk called Mikao Usui. Through deep meditation he discovered several methods of passing (transmission) Chi from one person to another by the act of initiation, invocation and touch. Dr Usui created a separate form for those in the outside world from those in the monastic life, as the needs and awareness required were different.

Sandi Leir-Shuffrey comes from a short line of Masters direct from Usui who were trained in Usui Shiki Ryoho – the Usui System of Natural Healing. This is a unique system that puts aside the mind and personality and applies the simplicity of hands-on, non-invasive, non-intrusive touch to assist the receiver in feeling energy balance for themselves. This can only happen once their mind quietens, emotions calm, and their body relaxes to receive the reconnection and reawakening willingly.

Reiki means 'universal life force'. It is not a religion, nor is it contradictory to any religion because by nature it is universal. It is merely a force that we cannot be without. It is in the air yet it is not the air; it is in the water yet it is not the water; it is in the heart yet it is not the heart. It is ever present in an unlimited supply, constantly in motion and change. It runs through us at all times. It radiates from our hands as the power of giving and receiving.

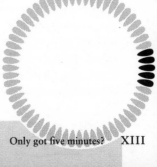

To have a clear access to the endless source of this creative, intelligent force, a simple process was created by Dr Usui to enhance its presence and awareness in us through initiation. Initiation is the vital key that separates Reiki's power and simplicity from other forms of healing and therapy. It is an essential part of the system in order to receive the transmission of energy, and must be given by a fully trained, qualified and registered Reiki Master. You cannot self-attune. Even the Buddha himself stressed the importance of the Master, who has trodden the path, as the one to guide you. Be sure that the Master you choose has trodden the path to guide you in safety.

The initiations usually take two days but may be shorter in cases of emergency. Once the initiations are received, this book can be used as a reference manual, a complete learning tool or a cross-reference to your other training. It details the series of postures used for self-treatment and for healing others, it explains the applications of Reiki and also provides the information necessary to understand Reiki as a spiritual as well as practical form. It covers the process of Reiki learning from Reiki Level 1 (the first two-day course) through to Reiki Master Level 2 – a process of apprenticeship that can take many years.

Anyone can learn Reiki, whatever their level of practical ability, mental intelligence or confidence of self. It is a very simple and harmless process. It is not necessary to give anything up or eat a special diet. Gradually, through regular self-treatment, Reiki shows us that we make our own choices of habit, so detrimental habits fall away as consciousness awakens and we become aware of our responsibility for those choices, a simple knowing of what is right for us at this time. It creates a waking up to our individual reality, at which point we can choose to change if we wish. Reiki restores the sense of self-worth. It gives back a sense of purpose, a way to remain centred and clear thinking, a way to prevent the accumulation of stress. It is used safely and effectively for all manner of conditions: to relieve pain; heal wounds; mend bones; bring about digestive balance; help combat food allergies and eating disorders. It has also been found to help relieve the side-effects of medication and serious diseases such as diabetes, high blood pressure, cancer, etc. It can access energy for a growing foetus and its mother and be applied for pain relief during labour. It assists the healing of sports injury and lessens emotional stress. It can lift the spirits and give confidence when there is a lack of direction, general unhappiness or depression. Not only does a physical healing take place, but there is also a change in mental attitude and emotional calming. Reiki heals the longing heart.

The principle of simplicity promoted by Reiki allows us to let go of our head clutter, our endless longing and desire for more, and come back into balance. When resting in the state of being, in a present and unaltered state, we can feel the love.

10 Only got ten minutes?

Reiki is a popular system of hands-on healing that is as current today as it was in the nineteenth century when it was devised.

History

The origins of Reiki have been traced back to Buddhist Sanskrit Scriptures. It is believed that the earliest form of Reiki was used by Buddhist monks in a different way from today, as part of the intricate system of prayer, invocation, ritual and surrender needed for life as a monk, most probably limited to self-treatment. It was a completely Holy focus: a self-addressing hands-on system to change the flow of Chi energy in the body to become of a more Divine nature, holding the body and mind still with the hands while the focus remained on the inner coursing of the Chi. In 1979 a silk book was unearthed in China that dates from as early as 206 BC. It is called Dao Ying Qi Fa – Method of Inducing Free Flow of Chi. It contains 44 drawings of Chi Gong postures, some of which were an essential part of the training in the Shaolin Temple in Henan. It is believed that the Art of Reiki was a form of Chi Gong adapted and incorporated into the way of Buddhist Temple practice.

Reiki somehow faded from the practice of the monks as they focused more and more on the mind and spirit and less on the body. Our present-day form was rediscovered in the late-nineteenth century by a Buddhist monk called Mikao Usui. He discovered a way to activate the natural healing ability within the hands of each person, when he spent three weeks in deep meditation. Dr Usui discovered some sacred symbols in the spiritual scriptures in Japanese Buddhism that were the keys to unlocking this magnificent, practical system. His original aim was to provide a way to help individuals take control of their own health and well-being and thereby become healthier and happier. He found that by placing the hands on a person who was unwell they regained their strength and the pain subsided. He put together a simple process of hands-on positions that cover the whole body, as he was applying the healing to the person and not the symptoms. He saw the symptoms as the body's way of telling the person that they needed to look at their lifestyle, their dietry habits and their attitude, which were producing negative energy in the body and forming illness. He created a separate form for those in the outside world from those in the monastic life, as the needs and awareness required were different.

Practice

The word 'Reiki' is the Japanese for 'universal life force' – the energy within us and around us. In times of stress, injury or emotional distraction, the flow of this energy is interrupted or blocked in some way. Reiki is the simplest of healing systems as it can be learnt in a short two-day course in which the energy is activated by the Reiki Master, and both self-healing and the healing of friends and family are taught. Once learnt, Reiki never leaves and becomes an easy-to-use and practical way to help in everyday life.

Taking responsibility for one's own well-being gives independence, strength and the clarity needed to be a better partner, parent or friend. Reiki is accessible to all people and does not require any special ability or any prior knowledge of the workings of the body, illness or health matters.

The most important aspect of this technique is the still and silent environment in which Reiki is practised that creates the stillness and quietness in the mind and heart of the receiver. Reiki offers valuable time out from the mad rushing world which we continually try to catch up with. Everyone needs time to stand still, reflect, relax, release and unwind, and enjoy the moment. People sometimes find themselves becoming content with less and happier with what they already have, with the added ability to change that which they no longer need.

During a treatment the client lies down, fully clothed, and closes their eyes. The practitioner places their hands directly on the major parts of the body, gently holding them still for about two minutes in each position, starting from the head and working down the front and then the back of the body. During this time the hands apply energy to all the major areas of tension and organs within the body that govern the hormone system and the eliminatory system. The body draws the Reiki through the practitioner's hands to wherever it is needed and releases deep tensions that have been stored over the years.

The treatment takes about an hour – or 10 to 20 minutes for a full self-healing – and ends with a technique to awaken the person while still maintaining the deep calm experienced. Having the hands actually touching the body is an important part of the Reiki system as this creates a feeling of safety, trust and a connection to the world.

The access to this energy is created during the attunement process. The attunement is given by the Reiki Master on the Reiki First Degree class, and the practitioner thereafter becomes a conduit rather than the director of the force. The energy naturally has healing ability. It is drawn to wherever it is needed in the body by the body's own inherent wisdom. Just as the body will tell you when you are ill it will also tell you when recovery has happened, as you will feel good again. The anxiety or struggle will be replaced with joy and ease.

Reiki First Degree is a two-day course that gives the ability to activate this energy for use on oneself, friends and family. We can use it safely on children, the elderly and even pets. The Reiki Second Degree is held over three or four sessions and includes in-depth mental and emotional balancing, healing from a distance and applying energy to situations and concepts.

It is possible to teach yourself a great deal about Reiki from a book such as this one, but in order to gain the full experience and the energy activation for yourself it is necessary to receive this process from a qualified Reiki Master (teacher).

Mastery

Reiki Master's Level 1 is for mastery over oneself, taking your own relationship with yourself to another level. It involves further activation and meditation techniques that relax the body and awaken awareness. Reiki Master's Level 2 is the teacher training apprenticeship and cannot be undertaken unless the student has been in professional practice for at least two years. It is traditional to be invited into this role by the initiating Master.

Reiki is learnt by all kinds of people, from doctors, nurses, psychiatrists and complementary practitioners to everyday people such as you or I. It integrates so beautifully within each system and enhances all other treatments. It has been found that when the mind and body are still, the natural healing in the body is triggered. So, whatever other treatment is necessary for our condition, it complements and helps the individual regain that essential vitality needed for a good recovery and then maintain the state of good health. A strong constitution is able to yield to the stresses of life and stay strong. There is no reason for us to deteriorate as we get older if we put that bit of effort into observing our lifestyle and seeing what may need to change for us to remain well and happy. Keeping up daily exercise is essential to the maintenance of the muscles, bones, the natural working of the body and the health of the mind.

Get Started in Reiki endeavours to answer all your questions prior to learning, but once you have learnt you can read through it again and it will seem like a totally different book. Once you have felt Reiki in your hands and seen it working in your life these explanations make more sense and give you the confidence to keep practising. As Reiki is an experiential knowledge, it is always best to simply lie down and practise the technique for self-treatment and allow your natural wisdom to answer all the questions from inside of you. Each individual knows what they need if they first take the time to quieten down the voices of the world and the voices of self-doubt.

1

What is Reiki?

In this chapter you will learn:
- *definitions of Reiki*
- *common misconceptions*
- *a little about the healing application*
- *an exercise on conscious breathing.*

As you think, so you shall become.

Rei – Universal

Ki – Life Force

Figure 1.1 Reiki Kanji.

Insight
Reiki opens the mind and the spirit to the causes of disease and pain and reinforces the body's ability to heal itself.

It is very hard to describe Reiki. It is as hard as describing the taste of a strawberry to someone who has never eaten one. Once the strawberry is in the mouth then there needs to be no explanation. Reiki answers all its own questions once the experience is felt.

I shall begin by briefly listing what Reiki is not, followed by what it can be. Hopefully by the end of this book you will have all the knowledge and information to enable you to gain some insight into what a magnificent subject healing is, but it is not until you receive the attunements for yourself that the simplicity, magnitude and pleasure of Reiki can reveal itself to you.

Reiki is not ...

- *an organization*
- *a religion*
- *a cult*
- *a dogma*
- *a mystery*
- *intellectual*
- *learnt with the mind*
- *difficult to learn*
- *something you forget easily*
- *harmful in any way*
- *complicated*
- *exclusive*
- *invasive*
- *a commodity*
- *channelling*
- *to do with spirits and entities*
- *limited in use*
- *cranky*
- *New Age*
- *inaccessible*
- *costly*
- *a cure all*
- *a moral*

Reiki is ...

- *Rei – Universal, Ki – Life Force*
- *transmitted through initiation by a fully qualified, registered Master*
- *light in motion/energy in motion*
- *love of the creator*
- *abundant and naturally available at many levels to suit the individual needs*
- *intelligent and creative*
- *the source of all things*
- *a powerful healing process*
- *empowering and self-empowering*
- *unlimited*
- *effective in chronic and acute illness*
- *a catalyst for change*
- *the harnessing of external energy to enhance the quality of internal energy*
- *constant*
- *dynamic*
- *transformative*
- *easily learnt*
- *easily applied for self-treatment and to family, friends and pets*
- *effective for all illnesses and side-effects of medication*
- *a balancing force of spirit, mind, emotion and body*
- *holistic*
- *the greatest pain reliever and healer of wounds*
- *a healer of the soul*
- *permanent*
- *a spiritual journey*
- *the application of spiritual power to bring about happiness*
- *meditative*
- *energizing*
- *restorative*
- *calmative*
- *expansive*

- *energy in perfect balance*
- *a profound experience*
- *a healer of hearts*
- *a true friend*
- *a gift*

Insight

Reiki is like a quiet cave where you can go to get out of the rain.

Reiki is an accessible hands-on healing technique that enables you to help yourself. It is a giving and receiving process. It opens the mind to an inherent knowledge and understanding of how the body is created, what sustains it and what destroys it prematurely. Its most immediate aspect is that of pain relief and healing illness. It is not until we have a physical problem that begins to restrict the way we live and what we want to do that we begin a search for a way of balance. For many people the initial search is at the doctor's surgery. Often we feel it is enough to take some medicine for the symptom and wait for the problem to be cured. But many times this does not happen. We seem to get worse or, at least, find no respite from the condition of pain. At some point we may realize that treating the symptoms with drugs is not the answer we want, especially when some of these drugs actually make us feel worse. We end up in a cycle of dependency on the doctor, the medication and even on the illness itself; it is who we have become. There comes a time when we feel, deep down, that there is an answer, a simple remedy for our condition. It is not until we begin to look within and see that we may be creating this condition in some way, or at least can affect it in some way ourselves, that we wake up to the possibility of healing rather than curing.

By treating someone else we are, in effect, assisting in the reclamation of their personal power. Reiki practice is like an offering, an extension of the vital energetic spirit, that is drawn through the hands. Healing occurs as an interaction between the energy body of the receiver and the unlimited external Life Force drawn in via the practitioner. The energy body, also referred to as the subtle body or the energy field, is the electromagnetic vitality of each individual person that extends for beyond the physical body. The energy field reacts instantly to any changes in feeling, thought or chemistry, expanding through relaxation that which has contracted through stress and tension.

Reiki heals the wounds both seen and unseen. It is therefore mystical in origin yet not a mystery. It is a simple power that we, as a race, have forgotten because of the incessant internal dialogue and our compulsive need for doing. Reiki is the Awakener. A light shed on simplicity. A way through the pain into profound understanding of purpose.

Reiki lessens swelling, bruising, bleeding and blistering. It repairs damaged tissue, scar tissue, tension and trauma in the cells due to surgery, replenishes the flow of communication between the nerve cells, and purifies the body by increasing the elimination of toxins.

Insight

Life is like an uphill struggle, climbing a mountain in the deep snow of winter. Sometimes you reach a plateau, sometimes you squeeze up onto the relative safety of a ledge and sometimes you find yourself on the edge of a ravine with an avalanche crashing down above you. Then Reiki comes into your life and you find yourself climbing with confidence in spite of the rain, in spite of the avalanche and somehow overcoming all the rocky terrain and reaching the top where the sun is shining.

Healing can be subtle and slow or it can be tremendous and instant. Whatever our expectation of it, it is pretty much guaranteed not to be like that. No matter what form the healing takes we are always pleasantly surprised at how close to us the remedy was all along. Sometimes the medicine is needed, sometimes operations are needed, sometimes our illness will not disappear as we would hope, but healing can still take place to give back a quality of life that is empowering rather than dependent. Through the following chapters I hope to give a view from all aspects of healing so that you too can understand. The proof of the pudding is in the eating, however. If you really want to know then you may have to try it for yourself. When you start to feel better in yourself then your mind can open to all Reiki's potential and all of your own.

Resonating energy is simply universal intelligence descending.

Joseph Rael, *Being and Vibration*

Listening Hands exercise – re-lax breath meditation

This is the most useful exercise I know. It is so simple and quickly changes how you feel.

Find a quiet room and a comfortable chair where you will not be disturbed for 20 minutes by the telephone, the children or the cat. Dim the lights and draw the curtains, even in daylight. Decide to put your worries aside for now. Without effort, notice that you are breathing – one breath in and one breath out. That is how it happens. When a breath comes in allow your mind to say the sound 'Re' as in relax, and as the breath goes out allow the mind to say 'Lax'. Do not force the breath and do not breathe to the word, rather say the word to the breath. An in-breath 'Re' creates a state of anticipation in the body, the out-breath 'Lax' allows all the tension to let go. After 10 to 15 minutes notice how you feel. How is the body? How is the mind? Is there a little more stillness, a little more silence? Use this technique any time you are in a state of stress, anxiety, nervousness, or when you notice that your mind won't stop.

10 THINGS TO REMEMBER

1 *Reiki is hard to describe so it is better that you take the opportunity to feel it.*

2 *Reiki is accessible to all.*

3 *Reiki complements medical treatment by speeding up the healing process.*

4 *Self-empowerment comes through experience, knowledge and understanding.*

5 *Reiki comes through you but not from you, therefore it will not drain your personal energy in any way.*

6 *An expectation is a disappointment about to happen.*

7 *Universal is made up of 'uni' and 'verse' which means 'one song'.*

8 *Everything comes from the same source.*

9 *We can experience the source and its creative power by being still.*

10 *People sometimes find that by feeling better their life seems to change.*

2

The history of Reiki

In this chapter you will learn:
- *the background and origins of this unique method of healing*
- *the importance of a pure lineage of traditional teaching for effective learning*
- *about the author's journey into mastery*
- *suggestions on how to keep a journal of experiences.*

Within you lies the simple silence; be quiet and listen.

Maharaji

The true story of Reiki is actually unclear, as the one passed down to me has since been proved to be quite fabricated. I shall begin with the story that was given by Hawayo Takata, who brought Reiki to the West, and follow with the latest research, possibly also somewhat fictional. Myth and legend abound in Eastern history.

It is believed that Hawayo Takata, whose identity is revealed in this story, adapted the truth to make Reiki more appealing to the West as a Christian society. This is how she gave it.

Dr Usui

Figure 2.1 Dr Mikao Usui.

At the end of the nineteenth century there lived a man called
Dr Mikao Usui. He lived in a monastery in Kyoto, Japan. It is said
that he was a Christian professor of Theology at Doshisha University.
At the time of the graduation of his students, Dr Usui was asked the
question, 'How, exactly, did Jesus heal?' He could not give a clear
answer as he too had lived on belief and trust in the Bible stories as
being true. He resigned from his post at the college and went in search
of an answer.

He studied many other scriptures apart from Christian. He travelled
to America and spent seven years in Chicago where he received
a Doctorate degree in Scripture at its university. He eventually
returned to Japan where he learnt the ancient language of Sanskrit,
with its origins in India, and began reading the Scriptures that
describe Japanese Buddhism. He spent much time with monks in
a Buddhist monastery reading these ancient texts and learning the
sutras and mantras. One day he happened upon something that
greatly excited him. There, in the Scriptures, was a passage on
healing containing a formula written in symbolic form. The monks
explained that their focus was on the spiritual aspect of healing
through Buddhism: as the healing of the mind and body were
not their primary focus, the symbols were no longer understood
by them.

Dr Usui knew the symbols were what he was looking for. They were the keys to the healing ways of the Buddha, Jesus and all others, yet there were no instructions. He recognized them as being very sacred and special. In order to understand them better he decided to use his experience of deep meditation to learn the essence from within himself as triggered by each symbol.

Symbols are very powerful tools. They are keys to unlock and give us access to other levels of consciousness. They contain within their simple structure the whole content of their form and the process which they activate. Dr Usui understood the symbols but not their form, so he took them with him into deep meditation on a nearby holy mountain, Mount Kurama. He sat by a stream with no food and placed before him 21 stones to count the days. He told the monks that in 21 days he would either have found the answer or, if not, they could collect his dead body.

The twenty-first day came and Dr Usui threw away the last stone. At first he felt he had not achieved his goal, but as he surrendered and accepted whatever outcome was to be, he saw a great ball of light rushing towards him. It seemed to knock him into another state of consciousness. In his mind's eye, as if on a screen, he saw each symbol in a golden bubble of light. He held on to each image until an understanding washed through him. When all the symbols had passed through in this way, they had burned themselves into his memory.

Dr Usui arose feeling changed in some way. He came down the mountain feeling surprisingly well and strong. However, he tripped on a rock, stubbing his toe. His immediate reaction was to put his hands there. He noticed how quickly the pain subsided and the bleeding stopped. He had begun the task of gathering evidence that something had taken place.

As he descended the mountain he stopped at a stall selling breakfast. The vendor, realizing that Dr Usui had been fasting, told him to rest and wait for the preparation of a special light meal for his delicate and empty stomach. Dr Usui rested under a tree. The meal was brought out by the young daughter of the vendor who was obviously in much pain due to a swollen tooth abcess. He asked if he could place his hands gently on her face and as he did so the pain subsided and the swelling disappeared. Dr Usui realized that something truly special had happened to him.

> Meditation in solitude is a tried and tested method of connecting with our inherent wisdom. Moses went in solitude to the mountain and returned with the Ten Commandments. Jesus spent 40 days and 40 nights in solitude in the wilderness learning the resistance to temptation. Buddha sat beneath the Bodhi tree in meditation until he attained enlightenment.

He spent the next seven years living among the beggars in the beggars' quarters of Kyoto but realized that they quickly returned to their old ways. When he asked them why they had not moved on with their new-found health they replied, 'This is who we are, what we were born to be. It is all we know.' Dr Usui was sad but realized that healing the physical is not enough. A mental, spiritual attitude is needed also. So he began to teach the Five Precepts of Reiki.

Insight

You might not have noticed that you already have the universal energy in your hands. When you are in pain you place your hands there and the body's natural healing is triggered, making you feel better.

Takata's translation of the Precepts:

▶ *Just for today do not anger.*
▶ *Just for today do not worry.*
▶ *Earn your living honestly.*
▶ *Honour your parents, elders and teachers.*
▶ *Give gratitude to every living thing and every situation.*

The modern-day version of the story is that Dr Usui was a Buddhist monk living in a Buddhist monastery with access to the sutras and scriptures in Sanskrit. It is also said that he never attended Chicago University. Some people say he travelled in India and met Tibetan Masters.

It is more likely that he was a Buddhist monk and that Takata adapted the story to be accepted in America. The beauty of oral tradition is that it evolves but it evolves only at the level of consciousness of the story teller. Whatever the story – only Usui knows the truth – I have seen Reiki work. It is a definite power that works through the hands, and the transmissions activate this power without a doubt when performed correctly.

Dr Hayashi

Figure 2.2 Dr Chujiro Hayashi.

Dr Usui saw the need to look for people who would honour the teaching as precious and have the desire for change. He met a remarkable man called Dr Chujiro Hayashi who was not only a retired Naval Officer but also an aristocrat. Dr Hayashi was keen to assist in healing, having witnessed the destruction of war first hand. He was initiated into Reiki and set up a clinic in Tokyo called Shina No Machi.

When Dr Usui's life was drawing to an end he recognized Hayashi as the Master of Reiki and charged him with keeping the essence

Figure 2.3 Hawayo Takata.

of his teachings pure, intact and in their original form. Hayashi agreed to this and made extensive records to demonstrate that Reiki finds the source of physical symptoms, fills the being with vitality and restores the person into wholeness.

Hawayo Takata

In 1935 a lady called Hawayo Takata came to Dr Hayashi's clinic having been diagnosed with many ills, including a tumour for which she was about to undergo an operation. Takata had lived in Hawaii until, in her mid-twenties, her husband died suddenly leaving her grief stricken and alone with two small children. The grief created such illness in her that a tumour formed. However, when she returned to Japan for an operation a voice inside her said, 'There is another way'. She was directed to Dr Hayashi's clinic where she was treated every day for eight months, by which time she had fully recovered. She became a dedicated student, working in the clinic but not learning Reiki as, being a woman, she was not allowed. Over the years she showed a deep commitment to Reiki and eventually Hayashi broke with tradition and initiated her into First Degree.

During the Second World War Hayashi was called up to fight the Americans. Being a Reserve Naval Officer his first duty was to his country and therefore to fight. Being a Universal Healer his duty was also to heal all beings and see them as one. His dilemma was so great that he gathered together all his family and colleagues for a meeting. At the meeting he declared Takata would carry on the Lineage and teach Reiki as a Master, keeping the original form and essence pure and simple. He then said, 'There is no such thing as death, only great change' and left his body. His body fell back. He had gone into transition. The mark of enlightenment and lack of stress showed in the fact that his body did not decay as a normal body would. It remained unchanged for many weeks. (This also happened to the great sage Paramahansa Yogananda.)

Takata took Reiki back to Hawaii and introduced her gift to the Western world. She died in 1980 having trained 22 Reiki Masters.

The 22 Masters made by Takata were:

- *Wanja Twan*
- *Barbara Ray*
- *Mary McFadden*
- *Fran Brown*
- *Iris Ishikuro*
- *Virginia Samdahl*
- *Shimobu Saito (Takata's sister)*
- *Phyllis Lei Furumoto (Takata's grand-daughter)*
- *Paul Mitchell*
- *Seiji Takimori*
- *Bethel Phaigh*

- *Barbara McCullogh*
- *George Arak*
- *Dorothy Baba*
- *Ursula Baylow*
- *Rick Bockner*
- *Barbara Brown*
- *Patricia Ewing*
- *Beth Gray*
- *John Gray*
- *Harry Kubai*
- *Ethel Lombardi*

Wanja Twan

Wanja Twan is Swedish and lives in British Columbia. She lived for a long time with her husband and six children on a farm in

Figure 2.4 Wanja Twan.

Canada. She is a weaver and potter. One morning her husband came in and said, 'I'm off now' and left. For good. Wanja had a farm and six children to look after and was therefore very stressed by the prospect, but being a devotee of an Indian Guru called Muktanand, she had great trust in the Divine Gift. She prayed to her teacher to take care of her. Very soon she heard of a Japanese lady coming to the area to teach people healing. Wanja met Takata and a deep friendship was born. She was initiated and later became a Master before moving to British Columbia. She has taught many of the Tribal Indians Reiki and helped them regain their confidence in their history and self-worth. She, in return, has been privileged to learn from them Shamanism – American Indian healing through altered states, knowledge of non-ordinary reality, and earth remedies. Wanja has written a book called *In the Light of a Distant Star* in which she talks about Reiki, her closeness to Takata and of seeing dragons!

In the early 1980s Wanja went on a visit to India to see her Guru, Muktanand. There she was introduced to another devotee called Martha Sylvester. Martha was staying in the same Ashram and had heard of Reiki but was not going to pursue it until she returned to England. She was very surprised one day when her room mate came skipping in saying, 'You'll never believe it, there's a Reiki Master in the Ashram.' Martha was later initiated and eventually became a Master herself in 1985. In 1988 she was given permission to initiate her own Masters.

Figure 2.5 Sandi Leir-Shuffrey.

My journey to Reiki

My personal journey to Reiki began after many years investigating the metaphysical plane. At 16 I realized I was not like the other people around me. In fact I was so different that my parents sent me to a psychiatrist who sat in a rocking chair with dark glasses on and waited for half an hour for me to speak. I seriously wondered who needed treatment here! I taught myself to meditate (see Meditation at the Bottom of the Ocean on page 120). It came to me as a journey away from the surface madness and into a place of safe calm where everything made sense. After many years of trying to fit in to numerous peer groups and failing dismally, I learnt the Transcendental Meditation (TM) Programme of Maharishi Mahesh Yogi. This is a system of mantra meditation, and the use of sutras on a subtle level, including levitation, knowledge of other worlds, and access to cosmic consciousness. I spent at least two months of every year in the Ashrams learning the Siddhis, the Bhagavad Gita, the Rig Veda (The Book of Truth), listening only to the sound of Sama Veda (Songs of Truth, Indian Pandits chanting ancient vibrational sound to affect consciousness). I was there at the beginning of Maharishi's TM Siddhi Programme and practised diligently for seven years.

Although TM gave me a structure and a theory, in practice the experience I was looking for was still fairly random. I realized that mantra meditation was still working on the level of mind and I wanted to dive directly into Being. I became disillusioned with TM and the obsession with the technique. I didn't want to become a Hindu, I wanted peace in my heart. The TM Movement required me not to be myself but conform, not only to behaving like the others but also to wearing the same clothes – no make-up, flat sandals, etc. I wanted to be just me, a nonconformist Aquarian by birth, and so, sadly and traumatically, I gave up all my belief in The Movement. I am, however, eternally grateful to Maharishi for his wisdom and for giving me a good start.

In my search to be me and accepted as such, a friend introduced me to Prem Rawat, affectionately known as 'Maharaji', a 21-year-old Americanized Asian Brahman with a wife, four children and a dog. I was initiated into the 'Knowledge' of Maharaji in 1981. Maharaji began teaching Divine Knowledge at the age of eight and came to the West when he was 12. He gives a direct experience of God through four techniques, namely Inner Light, Inner Sound, Inner Taste and Inner Feeling. Reiki, to me, is the fifth technique – Inner Touch. I needed to give nothing except myself and a commitment to myself to maintain the connection. That connection is not dependent upon the technique, although enhanced by it. It is the ultimate relationship of Master/Student/Knowledge of God. This I practise every day and is my greatest gift.

In 1986 I gave birth to my daughter, Kim, which to me was the ultimate initiation of all, the chance to experience for the first time what Unconditional Love meant. While pregnant I began studying Rising Dragon Tai Chi Chuan and went on to learn short form, long form, mirror form and sword form Chi Gong, Push Hands, Ta Lu. Tai Chi is a Martial Art consisting of meditation in action and inner energy exercises. It brings about a deep understanding of Chi, energy, and the Tao of Other or way of others.

In 1990 I was 'Opened' in Subud – this is a form of spontaneous Divine Worship and cathartic purification. It comes from an Indonesian Sufi teacher called Bapak who realized that by practising his deep Divine Worship in the presence of others the energy would be transferred to them also. They would then be able to practise by themselves, even though group practice is encouraged as a support and as a more powerful process.

From time to time I investigate the way of the Shaman, having been taken through the 'Shaman's Death' by circumstance. For myself I use herbs, tinctures and remedies as well as stones and ritual, but never in my Reiki treatments. Reiki must be kept pure and simple.

I came to Reiki through my Tai Chi teacher who offered it as a way to assist our growth and understanding of ourselves. His Reiki Master was Martha, to whom I was introduced in 1988 and received First Degree. Having organized the class I joked that I would be a Master one day soon. I received Second Degree in 1988 also and began working with Martha, organizing her classes and assisting her with them. Within a year and a half I had organized the classes that were to teach 150 people. Martha was one of only about five or six Masters in the UK at that time and taught Usui Shiki Ryoho. There are now a greater number of Reiki Masters in the UK, but very few of them honour the original principles.

In 1989 I was privileged to meet Wanja when she came to Cardiff to see Martha. I arrived late and rather exhausted having just recovered from severe mumps. As it runs in my family to be early, being late was exceedingly stressful. I entered the full room rather sheepishly and hoped not to be noticed, but there was only one chair left, and that was in front of Wanja. It was my fortune. Wanja gazed into me with her endless pools of blue eyes and thereafter instructed Martha to make me a Master.

I became a Master in 1989 as I could not refuse an offer that only comes once in a lifetime, even though my life was in turmoil and change. I was about to have my second baby and separated from my husband at the same time. I began my two years of apprenticeship. I was initiated when six months' pregnant and taught my first class when nine months' pregnant. The apprenticeship was like the rock in a stormy sea. Whether I liked it or not, Reiki had to become my focus. Teaching appeared from nowhere and allowed us to move on.

I was thrown in at the deep end with the teaching, having never even stood up in front of a group before. I had to fight through my nervousness and learn to teach the hard way. Martha gave me the initiation and said, 'Let the Reiki do the talking'. What else could I do? I took many classes before I felt confident and safe teaching this subject. Today it is required that Reiki Masters study the Further and Adult Education Teaching Certificate appropriate to the country (see Chapter 11). I did, however, learn that Reiki can take you way beyond the limitations and expectations of yourself.

I underwent the Master Teaching Training while awaiting the birth of my son, Tallis, having somehow bypassed the three years of preparation due to my background training. I rekindled my interest in drawing, painting and the art of Seeing, having spent ten years since my Art College Degree Course running my own, successful, men's knitwear business. I am today a practising, working artist constantly investigating ways of seeing energy through light, form, movement and pushing the barriers of the known world. Since completing a Masters Degree in Fine Art at Bath Spa University, my work has matured beyond the figurative and relies on the art of abstract automatic writing to attempt to describe the awesome presence of the sublime. I create visual poetry on a large scale, maybe two metres square, to entice people to question and look again within their own understanding. The combination of all things makes me whole, but Reiki is the first line of defence in times of stress. It gives me the means to hold the physical world still with my hands, quietening the mind, calming my emotions and allowing me to dive deeply into the place of Spirit wherein lies inherent wisdom. Reiki is so profound, it reveals your true self to you.

Since 1989 I have only taught five further teaching Masters who each trained with me for over six years. I have begun the training of several others who have not managed the commitment or decided to skip the apprenticeship and learn in one day on the cheap. Reiki chooses its own Masters. Takata did not teach anyone else for over 37 years; now some Masters boast about initiating over a thousand teaching Masters themselves. There is far more to it than meets the eye.

Further thoughts

The issue of money and free training has dissipated the purity of the transmission by people's new theories. It is a shame that this system was not regulated back then to safeguard the principles, but evolution has let the changes expand and grow beyond recognition. All forms still like to ride on the back of the word Reiki as it has sacred content, even in the word itself. Reiki is combined with everything you can imagine nowadays. I am glad to say that I learnt a beautiful and simple form that is so complete that nothing needs to be added to it.

Some indigenous people pass down their knowledge in symbolic form without meaning but with pure subjective experience. This way the symbols or rituals are not open to interpretation by the ignorant and changed to be devoid of the Spirit.

Being initiated as a Master is only the beginning of the commitment. True Mastery comes about through humility.

Prepare for a life of sacrifice, not sacrifice of things you want and have but things you are.

Unknown

Listening Hands exercise – the personal journey

Keep a journal of your experiences. Note the times of synchronicity and coincidence. Catalogue events that show a change in the workings of your life. Write down your dreams every day, noticing when patterns occur, reoccuring dreams about the same place or same person. Note the symbols, colours and phrases said to you and by you in the dream. When you recognize that daily, waking life is no less symbolic than the dream state, apart from a few more limitations, you will begin to discover that your night visions teach you about yourself and your world. Guidance may be given if you look for it.

10 THINGS TO REMEMBER

1 *Practice is the key.*

2 *Experience removes all doubt.*

3 *Knowledge comes about through questioning.*

4 *Understanding follows naturally.*

5 *Respect creates a sacred space.*

6 *The only constant is change, therefore change is inevitable.*

7 *Peace is already within, waiting to be set free.*

8 *Keep everything simple and then even simpler than that.*

9 *Unconditional love comes about when you are at peace with yourself.*

10 *Non-judgement allows people to be themselves, warts and all; only then is change possible.*

3

The Reiki precepts

In this chapter you will learn:
- *the five spiritual precepts of Reiki that can begin to be practised in daily life to restore happiness and well-being*
- *about changing common sources of negativity into positive affirmation to bring creative being back into the present moment*
- *an exercise on the awareness of the present moment.*

If you want to know your past life, look at your present condition; if you want to know your future life, look at your present actions.

Buddha

- ▶ *Just for today I am at peace.*
- ▶ *Just for today my mind is at rest.*
- ▶ *I earn my living honestly and do harm neither to anyone, anything nor to the environment.*
- ▶ *I honour my parents, elders, teachers, children, friends and myself.*
- ▶ *I give thanks to every living thing and every situation whatever form it may take, for within it is contained my growth and understanding.*

I wish to focus on each of the Reiki precepts in turn as they increasingly become useful affirmations by which to live a happy and contented life. The more they are practised, the more real their aspects become in life.

Anger

Insight

Anger comes from four main sources: frustration, injustice, attack on self-esteem or the threat of physical harm. We deal with anger in many different ways but mostly it makes us feel tense and out of control. In order to transform the power of anger into a creative form of energy, we need first to acknowledge it.

1 JUST FOR TODAY I AM AT PEACE

This is an affirmation that creates the opposite of the state of anger. Anger is a condensed form of energy that arises through conflict of thought with either ourselves or others. Some anger is justified and needs to be expressed through assertion rather than aggression. Anger has its seat in the liver and is fed by medical or recreational drugs, alcohol and caffeine, impatience, intolerance, guilt, blame, a lack of either compassion, self-knowledge, self-awareness or Divine Consciousness. It is the element of fire, which feeds itself if it is not swiftly dissipated. Anger is a loss of control. It is a separation from our true consciousness. We then become angry and guilty at being angry in the first place. Anger passed on is a seed given to another. That which is not dealt with by us, in us, and with the voice of truth, must not be given away to another in order merely to pass on the responsibility for it. As anger is energy it will either be stored or transformed if we address it from that point of view. Anger disrupts the natural flow, creating discomfort in the head and solar plexus. Adrenalin is produced which stimulates the system, speeding it up for action. In order for it to be transformed we look first to the breath. Adrenalin-charged breath is fast high-chest breathing. Relaxed and peaceful breath is gentle, calm complete breathing. The pulse is slower, the mind is clear and still.

When someone makes you angry, remember it is *your* anger you feel, not theirs. It is within you, therefore it is only you who can change those feelings. One way is to change your mind, which is very tricky in this situation. The other is to change the physiology by becoming aware of the body, the breath, the heartbeat and making an effort to slow it back to calm. Then rational thinking is more easily accessed.

Technique for dissipating anger

Hold one hand on the heart and the other on the solar plexus (Chapter 8, Position 7) and give Reiki here as you compose yourself. This position helps restore emotional balance, puts out the fire and stimulates a chemical change towards love and away from adrenalin. Never apologize for justified anger as this gives the power back to the person triggering it in you.

If anger is a common emotion for you, lie down and practise the heart and solar plexus Reiki positions and repeat to yourself three times the precept of: 'Just for today I am at peace'. When you feel good, sit up and write down what it is that is really behind the anger. Read what you have written several times. Come back to it later when you are in a different mood and write down what you intend to do about it, coming from a place of compassion and peace. I also use 'Just for today I am in a state of forgiveness', for forgiveness is the perfect balance for anger but is not easy to give. Maharishi Mahesh Yogi has said, 'When you forgive, all nature enjoys your brilliance and returns joy to you'.

The results of unexpressed, stored anger are depression, anxiety, panic attacks, suicidal feelings, self-mutilation, eating disorders, substance addiction, blame and, the deepest of all, guilt. Learning what is really the issue by meditating on it, learning how to express it constructively and changing the powerful force of anger energy into another form creates freedom, movement, self-respect and love.

It is not easy to generate love when you are angry and, likewise, it is not easy to generate anger when you feel love.

> **Insight**
> Forgiveness is said to happen when all your anger is used up. Forgiveness happens when you no longer allow the other person's action to affect you. Sometimes it is impossible, however, if their action was actually unforgivable.

There is an old Chinese proverb that says, 'Embrace tiger, return to mountain'. The word 'embrace' is the way to deal with negative emotion, not to push it away, try to hide from it, deny it or give it to someone else but simply to embrace it and return home. We must refuse to have a war in our own back yard and especially in our own being. Peace begins with our commitment to being in truth.

Worry

> **Insight**
> Create distance between yourself and what creates distress by being quiet and still. Watch the world go by without comment. Be patient and let all things pass and you will become less attached to the stuff of the world and your own thoughts.

2 JUST FOR TODAY MY MIND IS AT REST

This affirmation deals with the mental preoccupation with unwanted thoughts known as worry. Some people are constant worriers and most of us have had the experience at one time or another. Thoughts go round in an endless circle trying to find a way of resolving circumstance. When it is realized that everything comes from the Divine Will, we see that all things resolve and change into something else.

Technique for dissipating worry

By repeating this affirmation during the practice of the heart and solar plexus position, 'Just for today my mind is at rest', we realize that it can be a possibility. When the mind begins to calm it also clears. The spinning cycle of negative, uncomfortable thoughts begins to leave us to feel a sense of hope again. From a position of stillness and silence our thoughts gather themselves again. It is useful to write down the worries before beginning the exercise and to wait for the stillness. It is my constant experience that when the stillness arrives so too do the solutions; write them down also, and read them over several times. Take another look later. Remember the principle that all chaos is simply change in motion.

Worry and anxiety are actually the emotion of fear, coloured with the knowledge of past experiences, fed with the imagination. Imagination is the possible future that does not, in fact, yet exist. The future is made from this moment and therefore has the chance to become whatever we intend it to be. Create it through fear and it will scare us, create it with clarity and it will magnificently surprise us. To release ourselves from the worry cycle we must begin to trust that we will be taken care of. Worry for others is futile as they have their own life to lead. Also trust that they will be taken care of. As Khalil Gibran says in *The Prophet*, 'children dwell in the house of tomorrow, a place where you cannot go, not even in your dreams'.

Honesty

Insight

When the mind is still there is no room for worry, when the heart is calm there is no room for anger. When you know that you create your own world, there is no place for dishonesty. Your work becomes a service to yourself and the payment for your time on Earth.

3 I EARN MY LIVING HONESTLY AND DO HARM TO NEITHER ANYONE, ANYTHING NOR TO THE ENVIRONMENT

It is not only essential to earn our living honestly but also to be honest in our living. This begins with becoming clear about what it is to be honest to ourselves.

Technique for becoming honest

By practising the affirmation 'I earn my living honestly and do harm neither to anyone, anything nor to the environment' three times during the heart and solar plexus position, it is possible to begin to understand the voice of truth that speaks to us only through the heart. Here we can question our integrity. The voices of the head are usually someone else's, either a parent, a teacher, the media or the local group mindset. How often do we answer our own questions from the head and know in our hearts that we are a little unsure of the truth therein? The heart knows the truth and will feel clear when we walk our talk. When it speaks we begin to understand its profound wisdom and remember that it is our true nature.

To be honest with ourselves is to face the simple truth. The body does not lie and so will tell us our level of truth in sensations in the heart and solar plexus together. Whenever the solar plexus is agitated it is signalling a lie either in our own behaviour or in that of someone in our lives. It is possible to feel deeply distressed and fearful when someone close to us, who may be far away in miles, is living a lie. Secrets and lies are detected in the energy field and are acted out by those who pick them up. It is possible for a deep family secret to manifest itself several generations down the line. Not being honest allows others to feel the discomfort of the lie in their physical body without being conscious of the cause. This is how a secret in one spouse can cause a serious illness in the other.

By holding the body still on the heart and solar plexus, the stillness reveals the true sensations of the body for us to begin to remember the signals of honesty: it is your conscience. Catch yourself when your voice becomes high and tense, catch yourself when you exaggerate or sink into 'poor me' attitude, look deeply into what it is you are gaining from dishonesty to yourself by these acts.

An honest living is one that does not manipulate or dominate others. Providing a service or product that does not harm others or the environment. Being clever in business does not mean we have to be dishonest. The most honest professions are ones that allow giving and receiving as a balance without greed.

Honour

Insight

Reality is mine alone. What I think, feel and see is real to me from my perspective. From where you are, those same things seem different. They are coloured by your imagination, your personal history and your experience. Although my reality is essentially mine, it is hard to grasp, as it is constantly becoming something else. If I know myself well then I will be able to understand reality as it passes through me without becoming unstable.

4 I HONOUR MY PARENTS, ELDERS, TEACHERS, CHILDREN, FRIENDS AND MYSELF

This does not mean we have to love or even like all these people but to have respect for them in their relationship with us. It is these relationships, however good or bad, that shape and mould our personalities, create our strengths and weaknesses and give us a raw mirror in which to see the reflection of our own nature. That can be very uncomfortable at times, but to see how we can be and also how not to be is very valuable for our growth and our increasing empathy and compassion for others. We must change our attitude from 'look what they have done to me' to 'look what they have given to me'. It is difficult to honour in times of conflict, but to forgive and explore the possible opportunities to learn will bring about the ability to grow in love.

Technique for acquiring honour

By focusing on the affirmation 'I honour my parents, elders, teachers, children, friends and myself' during the heart and solar plexus position, repeating it three times and letting go, the meaning of honour becomes clear. Loyalty and respect follow as natural qualities of the heart as we see that all people are our teachers.

Insight

For some people, honouring their parents and teachers may be very difficult, but the honour can be to look at how not to be, to learn and grow from the hand that has been dealt. Vow to be a better person in spite of the wrong that may have been done to you. That was in the past, now is the time to start again.

By honouring ourselves we create self-respect, self-worth and the desire for simplicity as we no longer feel endlessly dissatisfied with life.

Gratitude

5 *I GIVE THANKS TO EVERY LIVING THING AND EVERY SITUATION WHATEVER FORM IT MAY TAKE, FOR WITHIN IT IS CONTAINED MY GROWTH AND UNDERSTANDING*

Gratitude is the most humbling of all experiences. It creates abundance in life, especially when our attitude is focused on giving rather than receiving. As Maharaji says, 'When man wants that which he already has he has fulfilment'. It is only through gratitude that the fulfilment is realized. Gratitude is an act of self-worth, and by having a strong sense of self-worth, everything is provided for us. It is a form of magnetism. An attitude of greed comes about through a lack of self-worth and so the universe sends a mirror of that to us. No wonder life seems a struggle.

Insight

Giving to others often takes effort if it is not in your nature to do so. When giving, seek no personal reward but give just for the pleasure of others receiving. Then be ready to graciously receive from them so they too can enjoy the process of giving.

Technique for acquiring the attitude of gratitude

By practising the affirmation 'I give thanks to every living thing and every situation whatever form it may take for within it is contained my growth and understanding' during the position of heart and solar plexus and repeating it three times in the silence, we gradually repattern our hearts to respond this way. We begin to be thankful for every creature, every person, even the most obnoxious petty tyrant, and especially every situation, as even in our greatest trauma we are held by the hand of grace. As we emerge from a difficult period of our lives we look back and see how much we have learnt and how strong it has made us. Of course, we also have the choice to use the difficulties to reaffirm our unworthiness and weaknesses, but this affirmation will implant deep within the psyche and create the feeling before the deed. It is not an attitude of the head, an 'I ought to be thankful therefore I will be', it is a welling up from the heart. Sincerity and compassion can sneak up on us when we least expect them to, similar to a rush of

(Contd)

joy yet more subtle. When you know them, they remain always. The Universe does your bidding and fulfils desires from the level of Truth. Gratitude creates humility, humility creates the death of greed and fear, happiness returns as a natural state of being.

Just for today ...

I find this phrase works very swiftly during periods of mental over-stimulation, stress, worry or anxiety. Any aspect can be placed after it according to the need. Look at how you feel, write down your emotions in a list. Look at how you would like to feel, write this down in a list. Choose three words from the second list to add to the phrase. For an example, when feeling distressed, anxious and weak I give my clients the affirmation 'Just for today I am happy, centred and strong', or 'Just for today I am happy, safe and strong.' This is repeated three times during heart and solar plexus application of the hands, even if the person has not yet received the attunements but is coming for treatment. 'Just for today ...' is all we have; if we can change our attitude for that short time then tomorrow we can reaffirm the 'Just for today ...'. One day at a time is the best way to recover from shock, trauma and illness, indeed, we can do no more.

Practising these affirmations during Reiki treatment holds the new patterning deep within the physical, allowing it to assimilate and become real.

Look into how you are feeling – write down the key negative words. Create your own 'Just for today ...' by choosing the creative affirmation in balance to your current fears. You will be amazed. Reiki self-treatment then holds this new pattern deep within Being, allowing it to assimilate and become real.

Insight

When all the trees have been cut down, when all the animals have been hunted, when all the water is polluted, when all the air is unsafe to breathe, only then will you discover that you cannot eat money.

Cree prophesy

When you forgive, all nature enjoys your brilliance and returns joy to you.

Maharishi

Listening Hands exercise – noticing

Take 20 minutes off. Go for a walk in the fresh air and preferably in nature. Notice how much time you spend looking at the ground as the mind continues its incessant dialogue. Look up at the tops of trees, look up to the clouds, see if any birds are flying. Notice the colours. How have they changed since the last time you were here? What sounds can you hear? Notice how loud your footsteps may be or your breathing may be. Quieten them down. Keep moving energetically but quietly so that you do not scare the creatures with the noise of your distracted mind. Notice how far you can see and how far you can hear. Notice too the fact that you can still hear the sound of the blood hissing in your ears. Make a vow to come here more often.

10 THINGS TO REMEMBER

1 *When the mind is at rest so is the body.*

2 *Are you being honest with yourself?*

3 *Honour everyone as your teacher, even if the learning has been painful.*

4 *Live with constant gratitude.*

5 *When we give Reiki, we give up our ability to get in the way.*

6 *How you think affects the world around you.*

7 *All people are trying to live in spite of the burden of their personal history.*

8 *Self-reflection is necessary in order to become a better person.*

9 *The only thing that stops us is fear.*

10 *Replace the emotions of anger, worry, injustice and low self-esteem with gentleness and kindness. Just for today ...*

4

Principles that govern the original form

In this chapter you will learn:
- *the levels of discipline and commitment needed to transform daily life*
- *the principles of Usui Shiki Ryoho that create a practical structure as the basis to good teaching*
- *how to create a spirit-based foundation for knowledge, self-knowledge and confident practice*
- *an exercise to free the mind and spirit from chaos.*

To surrender to the Divine Will is the most advanced ideology in life.

Healing technique

In a class a practical technique for hands-on healing will be taught that will be useful in everyday life. This is taught to bring about physical, emotional, mental and spiritual well-being for self and others. The technique is not the form, it is a part of it. Many people today do the course in order to become healers. No one can heal anyone except themselves. They are merely assistants/facilitators to another. Awareness of the other levels of the form must be taught and understood.

awakening of the senses to the environment and the Divine
erein, a conscious change, a choice to learn and grow, for
chance, fashions our destiny. Self-treatment brings about
self-awareness. It alters the stressed state and we become more able
to yield in the face of adversity. Pain is often our route to freedom.
It contains a solution. There are no short cuts to personal growth –
two steps forward, one step back, so it seems. Even when we feel
nothing is happening, everything is still moving forwards.

Spiritual discipline

Spiritual discipline is an awakening to the Spirit as Being and its
interconnectedness with all forms. It is a purification, a falling
away of the masks that cause an illusion of suffering. Through it
an awareness of our own Sacredness becomes apparent. There is
no turning back once the path is undertaken. Once you know,
you can never un-know.

Experience through practice achieves this level of awareness, yet
it is not always at first understood. The attitude of patience is
gained through trust of the whole form. The initiation makes direct
contact with our spirit and is made tangible through giving to
others and self-treatment. The relationship with oneself improves
to a quality of love.

Mystic order

This is a community of people who commonly recognize the
Mystery of the Universal Energy in action. People who have
received the Reiki initiation naturally are a part of this. The mystic
order, however, is not mysterious. Reiki is our essential nature
from which we have become separated and hidden ourselves with
masks of anger, jealousy, greed and ignorance, etc. If God were
truly a mystery or a strange vision, then it would not be possible

for the experience to be revealed to us. There is no belief system with Reiki but there is a common experience of the gift of life itself. One breath in, one breath out, that is no mystery. It is all we are. When we know, we may sit quietly in humility, inspiring and leading others also to the Mastery of their Soul.

Initiation

Initiation (see Chapter 7) is a sacred ritual that creates a focus of attention. It is a turning point, a new way, a beginning. The student agrees to receive and gives a gift of exchange to create the gateway they will receive. There are four initiations for First Degree, one for Second Degree and one for Master's Degree. Each is performed individually in silence by a fully trained Master who does not interfere with the process of their ego and realizes the serious nature of this moment for the student. It brings about a union with the Reiki. It is a ritual of invocation and direction of the Light, an holy act of purification. The initiation in itself will transform as it changes the essential vibrational frequency of the student. The frequency with which the soul-self of the student operates is raised so that what is put out is in balance and harmony, therefore what comes back in circumstance and relationship is also in balance and harmony.

Oral tradition

This is the energetic transference by word of mouth and by personal instruction in the presence and under the guidance of a Reiki Master directly and individually to the student. The class form is the completion of the tradition, i.e. initiation, exchange, history, understanding, positions, questions and answers, inspiration. Oral tradition has currently been diluted by well-meaning New Age people who have 'channelled' from the dead Masters new symbols and instructions. If the form had not been complete in its simplicity then I doubt that Dr Usui would have passed it on as such.

Historical lineage

This is the line of Masters who have orally transmitted their knowledge to their chosen apprentice and student. The history is a description or myth of events in the past that link us to the present and inspire us to see others' lives and paths as symbolic to our own. It is an essential part of the oral tradition to know our roots and respect the original principles.

Spiritual lineage

Not necessarily the Historic Line, this is said to be held by Phyllis Lei Furumoto, as agreed by the Reiki Alliance of Masters based in America. The Lineage Bearer embodies the essence of the system and with great conscience maintains its purity, simplicity, and upholds to inspire others to their own integrity, as indeed I do. It is my understanding, however, that anyone who upholds the purity, the sacred tradition and the element of simplicity also bears the Spirit Line, as there is neither hierarchy nor individual focus in the realm of Universal Energy. Exclusivity of any part must mean deviation from the truth. I honour my vows and endeavour to uphold the precepts.

Exchange of energy

> **Insight**
> Can you imagine being able to remain happy no matter what is happening around you?

Money is an energy system. It is a paper symbol of an agreed quantity, a value, an exchange for gold. We constantly exchange this energy for others – petrol, gas, electricity, food, clothes, time, manpower, etc. Each level of Reiki has an appropriate amount of exchange which is enough to make people think about their level of commitment to it.

- ▶ *First Degree should be around two days' average wage.*
- ▶ *Second Degree should be around one week's average wage.*
- ▶ *Master's Level 1 should be around two weeks' average wage.*
- ▶ *Master's Teaching Degree is by invitation only and is around six or seven months' average wage for training and apprenticeship. This level is a lifetime's commitment.*

To pay 'bucket-shop' prices for this empowerment is to receive a diamond for the price of spinach, or rather, receiving spinach as you paid the price of spinach when what you really wanted was the diamond.

In America, Australia and some New Age centres in England it is possible to do all three degrees in three days. This is like giving a monkey a chainsaw to do the pruning just because he can climb trees. Proper, careful training is necessary with a long enough break in between to assimilate the knowledge. The time gaps in between classes is essential preparation of the student through regular self-treatment and self-investigation, together with the beginning of the healing process to the energy system. A level of stability is needed to go to each further level as the force is very strong. It may seem like nothing at the time but in effect it is everything in disguise. Some of my students have gone on to learn the quick way with other teachers to the extent of giving Masters level in one day for one day's pay under the pretext of 'if life energy belongs to everyone then it should be given for free'. Certainly, I do not own Reiki energy, therefore I cannot sell it to you for any fee but I value my time, my training, my experience and the power of the sacred. I also honour the student's need to cross some boundaries for themselves, poverty consciousness being the first. Of course, if someone cannot afford it and needs it immediately there is no obstacle. But many is the student pleading for a concession who drives off in their new car.

When money is exchanged there is an energetic transference. Many people think that by giving healing for free and teaching Reiki on the cheap they are doing humanity a service. They are, however, assisting people in being limited. The exchange does not have to be money. I have a lovely rose arch, a painted hallway, kitchen unit doors, etc., all provided by exchange. Each act was done with respect for the principle and an understanding of the sacredness of the gift they had received. Would you trust your car maintenance to someone who had only ever seen a pushbike? I don't think so.

Generally, a training Master must have practised Reiki for at least three years before beginning apprenticeship. This may in itself last two or three years. Once the Master is initiated they are still an apprentice as they gradually pay off the guidance fee. Once the exchange is complete the Master feels ready to hatch out of the protection of their own Master to become the graduate. Every class and person brings out a new learning for them. No training is ever complete. Reiki chooses its own Masters yet the current Master looks for certain signs in their candidate. Their true conscience tells them the right person and the right time. It is not a personal choice, it is the only choice.

There is a tradition of exchange in the history of Reiki but this is only money when in the realm of a professional Reiki therapist. Otherwise, with friends and family just the awareness of the gift and exchange of an errand run, a bunch of flowers from the garden or assistance in some other way is all that is necessary. When I first treated my parents, and subsequently taught them, the exchange they made was to lie down and receive, for parents can be constant givers, not able to receive. In receiving, you are allowing the other person to have the pleasure of giving.

The Reiki practitioner gives their time and dedication to the client. They have to pay the bills and feed their children. If healing is for free, then the client frequently does not participate in their process of achieving well-being, they can often leave it up to the healer to heal. This is not taking responsibility but passing it on to someone else, reinforcing their own weakness. They must realize that the practitioner is only the access for their own self to heal itself. No personal credit is taken for the effects of Reiki. It does itself.

Symbols

There are three symbols for Second Degree and one for Masters Degree. These are used at initiation. They are described more fully in the section on Second Degree form (Chapter 10).

Many other symbols have been claimed to be channelled from the dead Masters or spirit guides and called 'New Reiki symbols', but Dr Usui's System of Healing contains only four. Some say they use a fire symbol to create energy, but Reiki is pure energy and so contains all elements. Some say they use a Tibetan symbol for spirit, but Reiki is Spirit. Some say they use a balancing symbol for calming, but Reiki is the balance. Some use different coloured rays for different conditions and say that Reiki is red, but Reiki is pure light and therefore is all colours. Why divide and complicate that which is completely all-encompassing and simple? Spiritual materialism is the dis-ease of the present day, the accumulation of techniques and paraphernalia in order to impress the soul and the psyche. The soul and psyche just need stillness, silence and humility.

Treatment

A whole body treatment takes between an hour and an hour and a half. It uses contact and connection through the hands in a set sequence that is flexible and adaptable according to the circumstances. People who cannot lie down may sit up. The formula is a good guideline to follow. It has been carefully worked out to flow through the whole body without bringing the receiver back from their deep relaxation by the interruption of the hands moving. This is the grounding or earthing of the spiritual aspects of the form; the Being into Becoming. Holding the person in stillness and silence so they may see that part of themselves that is usually masked by sight, sound and the distraction of worldly activity. A scary place? No, a beautiful place. The giver observes the experiences of the receiver with interest and sometimes with awe and wonder as magic seems to occur, always giving gratitude to the force itself at the end and taking no credit.

The First and Second Degree classes are aimed at people who want to practise on themselves firstly, friends and family secondly, to improve their own set of illnesses, relationships and circumstances.

Insight

Life is like a river. It is everywhere at the same time. It is the source and the mouth; it is the eddy and the waterfall; it is the rain and in the teardrop. The river is coloured by what it encounters, but ultimately continues on its journey back to the ocean. There, in the ocean, there is no difference between the drop, the river and the ocean itself.

Learn to breathe and speak from the Soul.

Prem Rawat

Listening Hands exercise – clearing the clutter

To clear the clutter in your head and your life you must begin with your home environment. Sit down and make a list of all outstanding phone calls to be made, all outstanding bills to be paid, all outstanding things that must be done such as fix a hinge, mend a shoe, paint the windows, clean the hamster's cage. Take one room at a time and clear up the piles of things that accumulate around the surfaces. Begin to see them as symbolic. Your home is an extension of your mind – that can be scary! Take all things that belong upstairs up, now, and bring things that belong downstairs down, now! If you have a family then delegate duties to them if some of the things are theirs. Be ruthless in throwing out. You'll be surprised at how many bags of rubbish you keep hidden in every cupboard. Give clothes you haven't worn for the last five years to the charity shop. Throw away anything that is broken and won't be mended – like old cups and teapots without handles. Throw out anything over the sell-by date and anything you know you will never use. Simplify your life. All this clutter was once bought by you and brought, bit by bit, through your front door. You worked hard for the money to pay for it all, you spent a lot of your precious life working to buy it. That is why it accumulates. Don't be afraid to let it go. Finally, write a list of what you really want in your life and what you no longer require in your life. Wake up and do something about it. The weight off your mind will be even bigger than that of the bags of rubbish that will go.

10 THINGS TO REMEMBER

1   *Healing is wholeness.*

2   *Integration is the gathering up of disintegration.*

3   *We are constantly at a crossroad with the choice of direction.*

4   *Discipline maintains good practice and gets results.*

5   *Reiki is tangible, you can actually feel it in your hands and in your body.*

6   *The key to self-awareness is to focus on the breath.*

7   *Reiki works in spite of any self-doubt regarding your ability to be a kind and caring person.*

8   *First respect yourself, then you will be able to respect the Reiki and also your client.*

9   *Reiki is a transfer of energy; it will wake you up and then it is up to you.*

10 *In the presence of a more powerful force, we can take on the force as our own.*

5

....

The nature of illness

In this chapter you will learn:
- *why we get ill*
- *symptoms of the modern mind*
- *effects of disintegration and separation on the body*
- *how to recognize both the dysfunction and signs of a separated emotional self*
- *an exercise to quieten the mind.*

> *By stimulating pleasure through fantasy you are playing with the full force of unhappiness.*

Barry Long

Balance and imbalance

....
Insight

A course of treatment together with the learning of self-treatment produces tangible results whatever the problem.
....

Reiki falls comfortably into the category of energy medicine. Energy medicine works on the premise that consciousness directly affects constitution. It is true that illness can bring about complete transformation as it takes us on a journey from pain, discomfort and entropy to well-being by seeking assistants to help with this condition, whether they be people, herbs, tinctures, elixirs, chemicals, objects, ritual, religion or healing touch.

It is very commonplace for our pain to be so deep that we think it is us. We become the illness and thereby see no way of ever being free of it. When we are ill, on whatever level, every cell and every part of us has to become involved. When in the state of being the wound, rather than the wounded, a negative veil is drawn across our understanding that prevents us separating from the pain of the past, or even the pain of the present to see that another reality may be possible. We become weakened and vulnerable which in turn makes us view all other traumas, shocks and conflict through the same veil. Thus more stress/distress is added. If we expect life to beat us down it will. If we wake up to the possibility of renewing the way we see and feel then nothing short of a miracle will happen. We have all experienced the feeling that when we are knocked down life seems to really put the boot in.

Our pain can limit us so much that it becomes a comfort to us. It can be the excuse for lack of responsibility, inconsistency, disloyalty, and the perpetual world of self-blame. We can become a needy drain upon the energy of those close to us and, in a sense, feed off others' strength. There is an energetic condition known as the energy vampire. This is someone who tends always to be ill, certainly more ill than you, who talks in a self-centred monologue of pain and poor me, asking for help but not heeding your assistance. When the person leaves, feeling much better for having unburdened their junk mindset on to you, you feel completely drained and exhausted. In listening and giving you open your energy field to be drawn upon. Reiki strengthens the field to such an extent that you only give away that which you are willing to give, and that which is surplus to your own requirements for health. Self-treatment will be able to top up any overstrain in a very short time.

It is true that becoming healthy and whole opens up a new realm of responsibilities. It is true that when healthy and whole you can do most things for yourself. It is true that you can think clearly, respond honestly and your life works.

As long as pain is the opponent, it will follow behind, tapping on our shoulder when we are about to break free. The simple explanation for this is the Law of Nature that states, 'Whatever you put your attention on grows'. Run away from pain and it will inevitably follow. Run away from responsibilities and you will not be able to cope. Fleeing from pain builds up a cord of fear. Not only fear of pain but also the tremendous fear of the emptiness of being pain free. We cannot be well as long as we contain jealousy, anger, greed, resentment, envy or hatred.

Stress is the modern-day causative factor in many illnesses. Stress is our inability to cope with or assimilate that which is placed upon us. When in a state of stress we may feel tense, tight, full of thoughts, restless in sleep, that we have no time, tense in personal relationships, a fear of losing control, physical discomfort, lack of enjoyment, lack of fulfilment, negative emotions, anger, irritability, we have no time to practise techniques for stress management, we need medication to suppress symptoms. The body can take only so much before its energy begins to implode and we take to our beds. The body in an imploded state perpetuates itself.

Insight

You will never hear of someone who was tired from too much happiness. You will never hear of someone who was in pain because they were fulfilled. You will never hear of someone who was trapped by their own freedom.

When relaxed and well we feel expanded, loose, clear thinking, rested; we have plenty of time, we have good communication in relationships, controlled without controlling, strong, flexible, enjoyment of life, fulfilment, satisfaction, optimism, we can give time to the practice of techniques and habits to keep us healthy. The body in an expansive state perpetuates itself.

The difference between the two states is one of awareness and effort.

There need not be any guilt about the illness; guilt is a waste of valuable time that could otherwise be spent making changes. Grief, anxiety and worry exhaust the forces of the body. To live fully in the present will induce a sense of immediate calm and relaxed happiness. A friend of mine once said, 'If I get help and become well, I feel there will be a huge space in my life.' Attention to pain takes up so much Being that the fear of being without it is often so great that we would prefer to perpetuate the state by putting off healing until another day. Nowadays people are too busy being stressed to take time out to be happy.

The fear created by suffering is often the fear that it will annihilate us and we will die, and we always do in the end! It must be remembered that the Spirit is not contaminated by fear, as we are. It is unchanging, balanced and all powerful. It is only in our mind and body that the fear exists, and only in our heart that we can connect with the fearless place.

Our bodies are created from the combined energies of our soul-self, emotional-self and mind-self and the relationship of all these levels to the Spirit Energy or Universal Divine Energy. They are a reflection of our inner condition. We are not our bodies but our bodies are us.

To explain this further I would first like to describe these areas of Being as separate aspects with separate unique qualities.

From spirit into being – a summary

Spirit is infinite energy, it is everywhere. It has no boundaries but can become manifest.

Soul is a condensation of spirit. It is personal. It is also infinite, when healthy, and has no boundaries, yet it belongs. It is spirit focused.

Emotion is a condensation of soul. It is totally personal and subjective. It responds to the interaction of external forces with itself. It is connected to soul via the heart.

Mind is a condensation of emotion. It is dense, yet unseen, and takes on qualities of the earth plane, such as duality.

Body is a condensation of all other levels of being. Its density allows it to manifest as sensory substance. The bones are so dense that they do not easily decay. They contain the history of our ancestors. The body is a mirror of the well-being of soul, emotion and mind.

The nature of the soul

The soul is the subtlest part of our energy system. It is in direct union with the Spirit Energy and is formed from its substance by grace, love and intent. The soul is the part of us that we are constantly looking for and constantly longing for. That is to say, a place of balance on the level of emotion. We feel our soul very deeply when we are in love, yet we cannot find even a glimpse of it when we are in distress. Various experiences in life remind us that it is there, or maybe that it no longer feels that it is there. Sometimes we get so depressed that we feel we have lost our soul. This is because, in part, we have.

When we suffer deep trauma, loss, accident or invasion, the part of our soul-self that governs that emotion will separate not only from Spirit, but also from our body. As more parts of the soul separate, the being becomes vulnerable and weakened, attracting to it more imbalance with less resistance. As whatever happens on the energetic level also happens simultaneously to the physical, it is easy to see that disease can be caused by a weakening of the energy structure long before it manifests in the body as pain or discomfort.

It is very common to come into the teenage years to be faced with desperation, lack of direction and a feeling of total emptiness. During early childhood we generally feel we are being carried along by the people in our lives, and if we are lucky enough, as I was, to have loving parents who were always generous and kind, then our soul, in a sense, is held by them. Once we break free of that safety we feel that something is missing but no one can tell us what that is. We have to find it for ourselves. Not everyone is a 'lost soul' but we all feel we are looking for something at some stage. Our journey takes us further into the outside world as we find the entertainment, colour and promise out there irresistible. Somehow the jigsaw never quite fits. A deep underlying stress is fed by the race and struggle of daily responsibilities. It is a rare person who reaches middle age without suffering some form of deep tragedy, be it the death of someone dear, the abuse of their independence and space, an accident, or the ongoing difficulties of dealing with a debilitating illness. Illness seems to come from out of nowhere. 'Why me?' we ask.

The soul can only be repaired by us becoming conscious of it and using life's experiences as a mirror from which to see ways of becoming strong instead of weak, empowered instead of vulnerable. It needs to be reintegrated on each level of being and cannot be dealt with by itself. The mindset has to change to allow the level of self-esteem, self-worth and self-knowledge to be strong enough; emotion needs to be clear of impulsive, obsessive patterns and the body needs to be able to regenerate its light content for the integration to be permanent. As Reiki addresses all levels simultaneously this process can happen quite rapidly. So as we heal the subtle body (that is, the energy body), changes will eventually occur in the physical body as afterwaves, then harmony returns.

What does the soul feel like? You may know more about the nature of soul when you feel you have lost it than when it is comfortable inside you. Then you will recognize it when it comes home and becomes whole.

Symptoms of a dysfunctional soul

- *separation*
- *feeling 'spaced out'*
- *feeling isolated from the world*
- *self-loathing*
- *deep sense of grief and loss*
- *deep discontent and dissatisfaction*
- *an emptiness within*
- *desire for death*
- *fear.*

The nature of the emotions

Insight

The way you treat your money is the way you treat your emotions. Are you generous or mean? What do other people say? Are you secure or scared? Do you feel the world owes you something? The world gives you only a reflection of what you have already given to it. If you get little back then start looking for where you can give out a little more.

Emotion is the bridge between the soul and the manifest being. It is the gauge with which we feel when we have strayed from the path of our heart. Emotion is a spontaneous reaction to the external world yet is coloured by past experience. It creates a physical response, a sensation or sensations that can be felt in the body, observed and subsequently acted upon. The gateway to integrating spirit and soul with mind and body is emotion. The heart is at the centre of the spectrum and is the seat of love. It is only when the heart is healed that we feel whole. Only then can we live with love in our lives. Our inherent nature and our past experiences determine our feelings, yet it is how we nurture those feelings that allows us to heal. By allowing the voices and our listening skills to descend from the mind into the heart, wisdom can be heard in the sensations of feeling, and knowledge of how to act becomes clear.

Symptoms of dysfunctional emotions

- *behaving childishly*
- *whining and moaning*
- *depression*
- *guilt*
- *shame*
- *blame*
- *displaced or suppressed anger*
- *low self-esteem*
- *confusion*
- *deep unhappiness*
- *crying*

- *mood swings*
- *isolation and loneliness*
- *inability to have successful relationships*
- *poor communication*
- *feeling small*
- *lack of energy*
- *feeling lost.*

The nature of the mind

> ### Insight
> We feel we have entered a party where we know no one, not even the host; we don't even know who we are ourselves. When we take the time to discover who we are, then we realize that we are the host of our own party and all the guests have come to dance with us. In our sadness and confusion we had forgotten to celebrate.

The mind governs our actions, it instructs the body and emotions on the basis of its reflective experience of the external world. The reflection it sees is from a unique perspective of the personality of that particular person. The reality we choose to believe in at any given moment is the outside world seen through the veil of our past experiences and emotions, coloured also by what we choose to believe in order to be part of our peer structure and society.

The mind by its very nature is dualistic; black/white, this/that, up/down, here/there, existence/non-existence, happy/sad. Therefore it is easy to have one set of beliefs one day and to find out that tomorrow the opposite is true. Which one is true, then, if our mind can talk us into and out of both sides quite logically and rationally? Both are possible truths but neither are the ultimate truth, for that place resides in the still point in the centre of mind where consciousness becomes conscious of itself and remains neutral in all argument as it knows all things are of equal value in the realm of experience.

It is the veering from positive thought to negative thought that holds the body out of balance. When the emotions are triggered by the attraction of the outside world our mind creates a judgement on the validity of the experience and triggers off a chemical change in the body according to the emotion. If it decides the attraction is a good and joyful experience it will produce chemicals that expand the energy system, and create reactions in the brain and nervous system that make the body feel good. If it decides the attraction is fearful it will create a chemical reaction that stimulates tension in the body, discomfort in the solar plexus and a shrinking of the energy system. The mind can alter the body instantly and consequently plays a very big part in its healing. Healing is not just about the wound in the body; it is the wounded attitude that really feeds the fire.

Only you can know your thoughts, only you can tame the mind and choose which thoughts to discard. First, get to know your mind then teach it to cease, then you will know the meaning of repose.

Insight

Conquer the lethargy, boredom and fear that stands in the way of a happy future. Boredom comes from inaction and laziness. If you feel bored then get up and do something. Boredom feeds itself and grows. If your body becomes inactive you will slip further in. Walk out in the air until you feel better. Spend some time thinking about what you can do, make, or give, instead. It is essential to catch the habit and not have it in your life.

To tame the mind is a very hard task. Meditation techniques have been taught for centuries for attempting to achieve this goal. As the nature of mind is to feed on itself then we end up with a constant internal dialogue which is often based on drivel. It even goes on while we are asleep, creating another equally entertaining reality called the dream state. This state is no less real than the waking state, it just has fewer limitations and should be viewed as having equal learning potential for truth. To stop the internal dialogue takes a lifetime of technique, but to change the content from drivel to affirmation is easily done with just a little effort and will bring about a rapid change in the other levels of the energy system and the body.

When the mind is agitated there is a corresponding tension somewhere in the body and likewise, if the body is tense, there will be a corresponding agitation in the mind. So to withdraw the mind from that which excites and agitates we must first settle the body. When we still the body and allow its functions to relax, expand and quieten, then the mind can begin to follow down into a deep place of stillness, beyond which lies the level of consciousness we call transcendence. That is, a place of Being beyond the mind, or in truth, it is a place of stillness before the mind begins. It is not the empty screen onto which all images can be projected, but the light which allows the image to become visible. This place can be experienced through Reiki treatment as the body is given permission to be held still and the mind is also held still with the physical hands. Intent creates the form. Attention creates the experience. Thought is not predestined, it is a reaction to the impressions which are received in the present, thus it can be directed for benefit only if we stay alert. We begin with a state of excitation, gain control from within by learning to hold the mind still and gain perception of the true nature of Spirit.

You may wonder why the mind by its nature has to release such a barrage of negative thought forms that create a sickness in the body. Is it because, in our ignorance, we know no better? Or are we missing something important? Once we know that the body's pains are signals for us to remedy with changed thought patterns, calmed emotional responses and a Spirit-connected, integrated soul, then we can begin to take responsibility for our condition and also be self-empowered to undertake the changes necessary. What other living creature is aware of its own consciousness and the Divine Will?

To treat the symptoms of the body with chemicals, or to treat the symptoms of the mind with therapy are in themselves not enough, for the whole instrument must be retuned. Reiki initiation attunes the human instrument to a direct pathway from the grossest form, the body, to the subtlest form, the Spirit, by allowing us to bypass normal thinking through its meditative quality, bringing about profound change.

Insight

Encourage these words in your vocabulary, integrate them into your body and act them out in your life: smiling, laughter, joy, play, fun, mistakes, share, care, kindness, beautiful, love, bliss.

The mind is very powerful, it can create images, words, ideas and concepts, it can change chemicals and choose its own destiny, it can even trick its own master. What must be remembered, however, is that it is not just a random alien that has been transplanted into our head but it is a reflection of our being and the integration (or disintegration) of the aspects that make us whole. The mind is a part of the instrument that we have created from our conscious will to exist. Now we must get it under control and put it in its place. It is our servant; we are not its slave.

NEGATIVE MINDSET

Misguided beliefs:
Negative mindset

- ▶ *is catching*
- ▶ *is much easier to maintain than positive mindset*
- ▶ *gets you out of situations*
- ▶ *gets attention from others wishing to help*
- ▶ *is easy to create.*

Truth about negative mindset:

- ▶ *it is easy to perpetuate*
- ▶ *it keeps you limited and dependent*
- ▶ *it will not get you what your heart desires*
- ▶ *it is a waste of life force*
- ▶ *it will not bring you health, balance, happiness or joy.*

Symptoms of a dysfunctional mind

- ▶ *irrational thoughts*
- ▶ *irrational behaviour*
- ▶ *extreme negativity*
- ▶ *endless agitation of thoughts*
- ▶ *anxiety and worry*
- ▶ *voices in the head*
- ▶ *voices outside the head*

- *tingling in the back and top of the brain*
- *feeling that the skull has been removed*
- *unreality*
- *a belief that others must be right*
- *preoccupation with substances such as alcohol and drugs*
- *perverted sex*
- *obsessions*
- *fear*
- *anger*
- *bad habits*
- *egotism*
- *rage*
- *indifference*
- *lack of purpose*
- *intellectual pride*
- *materialism*
- *acquisition*
- *ignorance of the Laws of Nature and Divinity*
- *lack of will*
- *lack of trust*
- *revulsion*
- *timidity*
- *sadness*
- *lack of control*
- *mental illness*
- *depression*
- *paranoia*
- *mood swings*
- *suicidal thoughts.*

Insight

When you are in doubt, be still and wait. When doubt no longer exists for you, then go forward with courage. So long as mists envelop you, be still; be still until the sunlight pours through and dispels the mists – as it surely will, then act with courage.

Ponca Chief White Eagle

The nature of the body

As we have already seen, the body is a physical manifestation of all other aspects of ourselves. It is an electromagnetic generator. It is energy vibrating, just as the other aspects are, yet it is far more dense than those parts we cannot see with the physical eye. Anatomy and physiology are incomplete in terms of whole-view theory, for the energetic is a system in itself that enables the anatomy and physiology to communicate.

Our subtle bodies are constantly being influenced by the environment as well as by our personality, the atmosphere, electromagnetism of the Earth, weather, climate, seasons, months and hours. Even the aspects of the planets at the moment we are born influence our individuality, and the Moon has a hold over our emotions.

Insight

To enjoy life you must learn to see that both wind and rain have equal value to calmness and sunshine. All are essential to life.

We form our inner environment, our constitution, from the air, water, minerals, plant and animal life that we ingest, together with their corresponding electromagnetic vibrations. The balance between our external and internal environment creates our physical and mental planes. It is an interaction, a participation with our environment. The external has infinite dimension while the internal is limited by our physical boundaries, it is more dense and compact yet also subject to change. The incoming and outgoing energy must balance or there will be overexpansion or degeneration. Our basic constitution is created by our inherited genetic patterning and by our mother's diet before we were born, as well as her physical and mental attitude during gestation. Constitutional change is slow, expanding and contracting like a breath, while the external conditions change rapidly, being influenced by all other things that are in motion.

As we evolve we become more sensitive to the subtle energies and become affected by those outside fields that influence our own body. We begin to notice the effects of electromagnetic pollution from televisions, computers, low-dose plugs switched on, domestic machinery, light bulbs, cars, transmitters, general static and even satellite interference. Background electromagnetic radiation from the Earth is actually essential to our balance but this becomes blocked by the man-made electrical systems.

Our own system is undermined by the changes in polarity, weakening immune resistance and allowing stress to remain deep. Illness begins when the external fields produce a build-up of polarity change in the physical. The blood spirals through the system in a clockwise polarity in a healthy body, yet in one that is continually put under stress and environmental pollution, and that includes geopathic stress, it changes to anti-clockwise. No wonder we feel as though the plug has been pulled on our energy in illnesses such as ME, MS and depression. The system of healing called Kinesiology relies on the principle that when the energy quality in the body is stressed, the muscle energy weakens.

Insight

Debt controls your energy and it undermines your power. You think your house belongs to you but it is actually only the space inside that you are paying for. Lead as simple a life as possible and materialism will not get in the way of your happiness.

Reiki is all-powerful, it can influence the constitution and repattern our genetic traits, through release of present constrictions, to align with a more divine and conscious evolution. The balanced magnetism of Reiki realigns the polarity spirals in the physiology to normal. It has even been shown that bacteria respond to changes in magnetism and that they increase in circumstances where our energy is weakest. Any imbalance in the energy system creates an imbalance in the body.

The body is the grossest form of our being, the final manifestation of thoughts, actions and deeds into a sensory, organic organism that lives out the duality of the earth plane in a three-dimensional way.

Through the two dimensions of the senses – hot/cold, smooth/hard, in/out, here/there – the Being perceives three, as its own self is the third dimension of the constant, the midpoint, the central reference point. The body is perceived as solid because its vibrational rate is so slow that an illusion of solidity is created in perception.

The skeleton forms the most solid energy system in the body. It is the roots and the tree upon which all other functions of the body adhere. Our form is a framework on which we hang memories, feelings and experiences. Our consciousness tends to reside within the body itself when in ordinary states of reality. When in a state of integration, our being leans against the spine as we would a sturdy tree trunk in the forest. When out of balance the being tends to lean forwards slightly and into the energy field in front of the body. This puts us off balance and causes great vulnerability. Leaning back is the sensation we feel when we become centred. If your toes are tense and slightly grip the floor when standing relaxed then you may be able to notice how you are leaning forwards.

The physical body is made up of elements of the Earth – earth, air, fire, water and metal: earth – vitamins/fibre; air – breath/psyche; fire – heat/energy in motion; water – essential messenger; metal – minerals. All these are ingested in the form of food, thought and breath. The assimilation occurs through the intent of the mind and its ability to leave well alone to the body-wisdom. The mind can interfere with the chemistry through its interpretation of the external world and the need for a reaction to it.

The body has DNA, both in particle and energy, as a blueprint that has been passed down since time began to remind the being and cells into which order they must be energized to function well. The DNA is a double helix, an inward and outward spiral or vortex, just as all energy in nature moves in a spiral or vortex. The energy system must become balanced with and to the body. The energy DNA is the blueprint of the form.

An atom consists of subatomic particles, each of which is a vortex of energy, spinning inwards from the unmanifest reservoir waiting in potential to materialize into the dense, solid and perceptible, all connected in the unified field. Matter, it has been proved, is mostly empty space with a few particles and electrons bouncing around in it. So we can see the importance of addressing the finest dimension of our form in order to heal the grossest.

Dis-ease comes about from inaction of life forces within, therefore the remedy is action, otherwise we perpetuate the illusion of being in a finite existence of inevitable dis-ease, decay and death. Giving up death as our reference point we can focus on the now, on life and living, on what is in motion rather than what may not be. Death consciousness causes chaos and physical destruction. We must use Reiki to begin to spiritualize dis-ease in order to find ease.

We are all familiar with what it feels like to be ill, in pain or under stress. Many people see themselves in terms of body, pain and medication and must be steered towards the power within. It sometimes feels as if life is a fight against decay. We know what it is to be in conflict, to feel hurt, betrayed, to feel out of control. Many of us live day by day simply trying to escape from the pain and fear of illness and dis-ease.

Insight

If I feel pain, but nothing can be found to cause the pain, does that mean that it doesn't exist and I am therefore mad? If I am just imagining it, does that mean it is not really there when it still hurts so much? Surely, if I feel the pain, then it must be real, to me at least?

How many of us live life in a state of blissful peace, with happiness and joy as our main experiences? Who has stolen our tranquillity and repose? Or rather, who and what have we given our soul to without true reason?

It is time, once again to become familiar with the unfamiliar. To know that love, joy and happiness are states of being rather than acquired traits once suffering and pain end.

Through regular practice or treatment of Reiki, that still place can be remembered: we can become familiar with it as our ever-present, trusty friend merely by dipping back in every day. I say ever-present as it never really went anywhere, it was always just waiting for us to return from the preoccupation with our pain. Remember, whatever you put your attention on grows.

Reiki can affect all physical symptoms, pain relief being the most obvious. It has also been found that the skeleton realigns into balance during treatment; the cells enliven and begin to throw off dis-ease; blood pressure can balance from high or low to more normal; diabetics find they need less insulin. When people are under severe stress, suffer from depression or insomnia, they find that they can cope better without the need for medication. Colds, flu and general infections can clear more rapidly. In cases of injury, tissue damage heals well and broken bones mend fast and strong.

As the physiology awakens, the dis-ease lessens. Of course, other factors are also important to observe such as diet, water, air, exercise, mental attitude, but to start with a hands-on practical experience that has immediate benefit is the best place for a kick start, especially to the doubting mind.

The magnificent thing about wounds, whether physical, mental or emotional, is that they can heal. I shall repeat that: *wounds can heal*. Reiki assists and enforces healing. Those who enjoy their place in society as sick individuals beware, as you may need to be prepared to give up your status. Are you prepared?

Insight

Wisdom comes only when you stop looking for it and start living the life the creator intended for you. Seek wisdom not knowledge, knowledge is of the past and wisdom is of the future.

Lumbee, Native American

Some of us feel stuck on the treadmill of pain, medication and lifelong diagnosis. We accept our lot and rattle around full of pills like a tube of sweets. Others are not satisfied with the high level of chemical intake that seems often to be merely an experiment. We know that addressing the symptoms is not enough. We wake up through our strong intuition to feel that there must be a meaning to all of this, the pain must be saying something; how do we learn to hear? So if we struggle and fight hard enough and follow our convictions, eventually we are led on a pathway out, onto a pathway home.

Once we begin to get well, we may be pulled back into the mainstream mindset when we have temporary weakness. Reiki is a way to fight without a fight. It is a way to become a separate and strong individual without being isolated and alone. It has the capacity to give people a new unrecognizable life.

To be spiritual yet in the world we have to be fully present within the body, with all the circuitry resolved and repaired. Then we can function from totality and gain insight for ourselves.

We need to look symbolically at our physical symptoms. If our back is weak we must find a way to strengthen our support of and from others. If our heart is weak we must wake up to forgiveness and gratitude. If our kidneys contain stones we must soften our emotion and stop being afraid to show feelings. If we are going deaf we need to learn to listen. But all must be undertaken without guilt and blame, for with them come more symptoms. Forgive yourself and be determined to win.

Symptoms of a dysfunctional body

- *pain*
- *tension*
- *cysts*
- *infections*
- *fungus*
- *allergy*
- *weakness*
- *fatigue*

- *lack of strength*
- *rash*
- *dizziness*
- *digestive disorder*
- *weight loss*
- *skin eruptions*
- *asthma*
- *vitamin/mineral deficiency*
- *accidents*
- *lust*
- *injury*
- *need for medication*
- *operation*
- *trauma*
- *wounds*
- *scars*
- *loss of a part*
- *stiffness*
- *immobility.*

Other factors that affect us:

- *relationships – conflict, duty, entrapment, loneliness, sexuality, abuse, lack of communication, loss of joy, loss of respect, unacknowledgement*
- *work – relating, fulfilment, recognition, entrapment, slavery*
- *money – energy, debt, addiction, gambling, lust, stealing*
- *inherited – diseases, mental attitudes, learnt behaviour, negative habits, mannerisms, family secrets, lack of support, suffocation.*

So much is out there trying to beat us down, yet one simple solution covers all aspects. In stillness and silence healing occurs and self-worth is recovered.

> **When the force that binds your body is scattered, you are like a bundle of sticks untied.**
>
> Prentice Mulford, *Thought Forces*

Listening Hands exercise – centring through breath

At times when you feel un-centred, find a quiet place to sit away from the world. Place the index finger on the Third Eye – the point between the eyebrows and a little up. Place the thumb to one nostril and the second finger to the other. Place the tongue on the roof of the mouth. With the thumb, close the nostril. Allow one breath out and one breath in, then release the thumb and close the other nostril with the second finger. Allow one breath out and one breath in. Repeat and continue for five to ten minutes. As the mind quietens down place your attention on the contact of the index finger at the Third Eye. This is a good exercise to practise before self-treatment.

10 THINGS TO REMEMBER

1 *Reiki is classed as 'energy medicine'. It repairs our energy.*

2 *Take full responsibility for your own well-being.*

3 *Emptiness can be a lonely place or it can be filled with potential, depending on how you look at it.*

4 *Harmony comes about when all aspects of our selves work together without strain.*

5 *Effort and determination are needed to make the changes permanent.*

6 *Silence is available to you even in the heart of chaos. It resides deep inside and is always there. You do not need to be shown where to look but how to look within.*

7 *Acknowledge your vulnerability yet choose to be wise. This way you will transcend the chaos and remain happy.*

8 *Light, sound and temperature are all aspects of electromagnetic field. Experiencing them will clarify what Reiki is.*

9 *Remain in the present, as yesterday has already gone and tomorrow will always be tomorrow.*

10 *The remedy for unhappiness is first to stop, reflect and then to act.*

6

The nature of health

In this chapter you will learn:
- *simple, practical ways to regenerate and assist body/mind/ emotional health through everyday action*
- *the subtle changes in life habits that bring about profound changes*
- *how to rekindle love as a basis for healing sexual dissatisfaction and dysfunction*
- *an exercise to keep the physical, mental, emotional self calm during action.*

> *What are you willing to give up in order to meet God?*
>
> Caroline Myss

Why is it so hard to be a human being? Does the dog need a manual on existence? Does a rabbit? The difference between a human and an animal is one of perception. We think we know better than Nature – the animal would never be so egocentric.

Every seven years every cell in the body has been replaced. So it may take seven years for the body to heal completely. Certain guidelines need to be followed for this process to become complete.

If illness is dysfunction (disintegration), then health is natural function (integration). To take control of our own health and maintain it as we swim through the sea of experiences without sinking, awareness must awaken and focus be kept.

Breath and exercise

The Breath is the key to all of the mysteries.

Joseph Rael, *Being and Vibration*

Breath is vital, it is our vitality. Breath, or Prana as it is known in Indian Yoga systems, is the vehicle for Divine Knowledge. Oxygen is its messenger. We are fortunate that breathing does itself as otherwise we would forget. It is our first contact with the world when we become independent from our mother host. It is our introduction to our relationship with the Divine Will. A yogi measures his life in numbers of breaths rather than numbers of years. Thus stressed, rapid, shallow breathing causes early demise whereas complete, conscious, purifying breath causes longevity. In India, breath is taught as a science called pranayama. It is through controlled conscious activity of the breath that different states of being are obtained and different states of health ensue.

We interrelate with other beings and life forms on the Earth by the connection through our breath. That which we eliminate is taken up by plants and transformed into that which we need to breathe in. When we can let the breath breathe us, we are relaxed and open to our intuition. Shallow and rapid breathing causes mental agitation, likewise mental agitation causes shallow or rapid breathing. During periods of stress or depression it is possible to breathe hardly at all, perpetuating the toxic, inert state that leads to entropy. The body is starved of oxygen and vitality.

An imbalance in the gas levels of the brain creates imbalance in the thought processes, reactions and ability to cope with stress. The purpose of breath is to draw in oxygen and expel carbon dioxide, to draw in life and expel that which is no longer needed.

Insight

To every human being, every single breath is important and every moment is precious. How many of us take the time to think about it and really appreciate that the breath and the moment is all we truly have? Be still a while, notice the breath as it comes and goes without you even thinking about it, and appreciate every moment as being precious, for soon it will be gone forever.

Exercise in a fresh, pollution-free atmosphere is the quickest way to revitalize energy to a depleted system. Exercise itself helps to free toxins which may be eliminated more rapidly as the metabolism speeds up. It also increases the dimensions of the lungs, allowing the full breath to have greater capacity. Stamina and endurance come about through less effort. The resting state of the lungs creates deeper oxygenation. Exercise turns the inertia and entropy into substance of useful density such as muscles and bones – the storehouses of power and motion. Exercise also strengthens the function of organs and boosts the immune system. The exercise machines at my gymnasium chant 'strong body, strong mind'. Twenty minutes per day in fresh air is recommended for maintaining general health.

Reiki self-treatment on the heart and solar plexus positions creates a focus on the breath in a position of restful alertness. We can then become conscious. During the restfulness of treatment, the breath naturally becomes slower and more full. Vitality then enters the cells as they open up to receive. A natural state of balance returns and is usually felt as peaceful joy or bliss. Bliss is a lovely word that does not describe an emotion but a state of being. When the bliss state is reached it is a recognition of the fulfilment of longing.

Water

Water is crystallized light which produces physical light as well as spiritual light.

Joseph Rael, *Being and Vibration*

A large percentage of the body is water, yet we habitually replace it with tea/coffee/cola/sugary drinks. Water is the container of messages. It is the vehicle for electricity and healthy function of not only physical cells but the fluids that move around the body and the emotions that govern the instrument. When we drink energized water such as natural spring or mineral water, our energy fields lighten and expand.

Fresh spring water has more vitality than tap water. Tap water has more vitality than boiled water or water containing any other substance. When other substances dissolve in water it ceases to be the power of itself and takes on the messages of the contained chemical substances. Coffee is toxic and therefore the whole cup including the water is contaminated with toxic messages.

Water is vital for cleansing, detoxifying and eliminating other substances. It is filtered through the kidneys (the seat of all emotion, grief and tears). Whenever Reiki is applied to the body, toxin release is increased so water becomes a prerequisite to help flush these away. It is the burden of toxins that weakens the system and thereby their elimination through treatment that brings back its strength. Water is the element of healthy bodily function and release. Water is vital for the healthy function of the processes of urination, sweating, out breath, tears, salivation – the processes of purification. When the vehicle is distorted by contamination then the messages are not clearly sent through the nervous system. Just a sip of water, or even the visualization of being in water, will restore electrical balance and reduce the fatigue of stress.

Light

> *[the] Creator made their bodies:*
> *Their hands of the 'Spirit of Light' and the 'Spirit of*
> *Manifesting'. From these two Spirits came first woman and*
> *first man.*
>
> Joseph Rael, *Being and Vibration*

Light is the source of all energy on Earth – it is absorbed by plants
which are then eaten by animals, it is transposed during biological
and chemical changes within organisms into other forms of vibration.
Fundamentally all things require an influx of energy to remain in
existence. With light we can see clearly, we are warmed, we are fed.
Light affects the brain chemistry to produce the sense of happiness. In
countries where the days are short people often suffer from an illness
called SAD – Seasonal Affective Disorder: the remedy is daylight.
Daylight can turn around depression, anxiety and grief. When holiday
time comes there is a mass exodus to the nearest beach where we can
bask in the sun and regenerate our tired, worn batteries.

Reiki is light in motion; it can be seen by some as colours pouring
out through the hands affecting the light colours of the body. That is
why we feel so marvellous during and after treatment. Our hearts are
lightened, our minds are cleared and the body's heaviness disappears.
When we lighten up we are happy.

Food

Insight

Pay attention to what you put on your plate and what
you put in your mouth. The food on your plate is the
body of tomorrow. Your food is the best medicine. If it has
no vitality, it may even kill you. Do you want your body to be
fat, lifeless and inert or colourful, strong and energetic? Make
small changes, working towards a rainbow diet full of all the
nutrients a person will ever need. You will feel better for it.

We can change to a lighter, fresher, more varied diet that contains direct life force. Energy from the Sun is stored in plant cells together with elements of the Earth that create the vitamins and minerals we need to create our own complex organism. If we eat fresh, raw or lightly cooked food, we take in the liveliest source of energy. We need less food as all we eat contains vitality. The tendency in the Western diet is to overeat, especially dairy products and refined carbohydrates. It is a misinterpretation of the body's calling for more energy. It is not calling for more food but simply more energy. So a smaller quantity of higher vitality food will satisfy the body, keep the structure strong, produce less waste and stagnation and reflect on the mental and emotional well-being also. Processed food, refined carbohydrate, sugars, pre-cooked, frozen or microwaved foods all contain depleted life force.

Kirlian photography of refined, processed food shows very little life force at all, so you can see why the body craves so much of it. Hence the obvious high rate of illness in the fast food era when we are all too busy to wash our own vegetables. A quick burger and chips washed down with cola contains hardly a trace of vitality. It contains bulk but does not feed or regenerate the breakdown of tissues.

A living energetic system must be fed with fresh living energy, otherwise entropy and inertia move in. The mind becomes dull and depressed, and life feels like pushing treacle up hill. We are so saturated with sugar and acid-forming foods that the electrical currents no longer provide an open frequency of communication from which conscious experience is gained. It has become a vicious circle.

It is no coincidence that most Indian sages and modern-day gurus eat a vegetarian diet consisting mostly of whole grain, fruit, vegetables, vegetable protein, a small amount of fat and little sugar or dairy. It is not part of a fad but becomes an essential refinement of consciousness. Gradually, as Reiki works on the system, it is possible to give up the need for stimulants such as tea, coffee and alcohol, give up the density of meat and dairy and the heaviness of processed food. It doesn't mean that everyone must be vegetarian or that if you drink coffee and eat meat you cannot be either well or enlightened because it is down to the basics of consciousness on the level of being. An Eskimo would find it a big problem being vegetarian but that doesn't exclude him or her from the experience of peace, health, love and happiness. Come as you are and see what you may become.

Rest

Resting became the living, inner vitality of the self within, bonding with power.

Joseph Rael, *Being and Vibration*

To rest is to stop but to remain conscious of stopping. To allow the body's neuromuscular tensions to return to ease. To give the body a chance to recover and the internal dialogue a chance to cease.

Dream essence of life is what heals life.

Joseph Rael, *Being and Vibration*

Rest – in the form of sleep and dream – should be regular and enough to awaken fresh not tired. In sleep the subconscious is allowed to play in the realms of dreams and many deep anxieties can be digested in the imagery or REM (rapid eye movement) sleep. The well-known Indian sage, Patanjali, said that 'Sleep is the psychic condition that rests our mind state, all material things being absent'. Write down your dreams in a dream journal. Look back over them from time to time and see what messages are coming up. It is possible to shape shift into any one of the characters in a dream to view it from another perspective. In sleep the body can slow down, recover and repair itself. Tension is relieved.

Insight

When there comes a time to desire to be well, all help is at hand. You cannot help an addict until they are ready to be helped. Each person has their own journey and it is not for us to make that journey for them. You cannot wake a person up if they prefer sleeping.

Rest – wakeful, conscious rest – is as important as sleep; meditation, resting the mind, relaxation of the body and being still without distraction on the surface. Rest to music is good yet rest in stillness is best. Reiki self-treatment is the perfect tool and perfect excuse to be still. The regeneration is far more subtle when in wakeful rest than in the rest of sleep. It is a chance to listen to the body.

There are states of restful balance in the body that are natural and normal. The body will return to these inherent states once stress and tension are no longer the main force. This relates not only to the structure of the body but also to the constitution.

During illness the structure of the body contracts, becoming vulnerable and weak. The organs become congested, the lungs cannot fill fully, the intestines become stagnant and general vitality diminishes. The pressure of blood increases as it struggles to complete its cycle without freedom of energy. Mental balance also moves away from natural rest and clarity.

The body's natural balance of wisdom cannot be maintained with drugs, it has to have awareness. Posture is an integral part of the body's health. The well person is upright, expansive and relaxed with resting energy at the ready to become – become thoughts, actions, movements, etc. The sick body constricts all natural capacity for freedom. Through Reiki treatment the deep relaxation addresses all levels of structure – muscles, tendons, ligaments, cells and bones – opening and inviting the remembering of a state of being unfamiliar to modern man. Harmony can only be rekindled in balanced rest.

Equilibrium can be maintained in the face of adverse forces only when the body, mind and being are strengthened through relaxation into a state of yielding. Yielding does not mean becoming victim; it means becoming flexible. Like barley in a field when the wind blows, we yield to the force in restful alertness without resistance and thereby bounce back with least effort.

Love and sexuality

Insight

Life without love is pointless. Personal love is concentrated universal love. The word universe is made up from 'uni' meaning one and 'verse' meaning a song – one song. Love needs expression in order for you to be able to feel it grow within you.

Love is freely available. That doesn't mean sex, it means the experience of love as a state of being. Without love, human beings barely exist. Without love, many perish and die. Love is an expansive force that heals the soul via the heart.

Through the experience of love itself, not love for something or someone, we can be free. Love of others is an incredibly deep and passionate experience and vital need, yet it always contains the possibility of disappointment and let down. That is probably what makes it so wonderfully raw and compulsive. Love is longing for itself. It looks for a mirror to remind it where it resides. But the mirror is just a mirror, it is not love itself. For that already existed within us. The experience of love is always within us in the place where personality and Spirit meet. It is always waiting for us to put aside our pain, grief and fear by making it our priority.

Being in love with love itself is as hard to comprehend as being conscious of consciousness. It can be given only as a quality when the dreams and phantoms of our created perception cease.

Anything is possible. A murderer can become a saint, a dying person can come alive again, sorrow can be lifted into joy. The change involved in becoming well creates a fear of the unknown. For some this terror prevents their recovery, for others it becomes an exciting challenge. The future is an unknown quantity. It is an uncharted land. It can be seen as an enormous black, empty void containing no hope, love, interest, acknowledgement or freedom from suffering, or it can be an empty space containing the full potential of all things. A vast field of as yet untapped energy on which we can impress our desires and create absolutely anything.

If we feel damaged in some deep way and are resigned to life never being anything better because 'they did it to us' or 'it's too late now' then at present we cannot be helped. But if we feel damaged, yet also see the possibility to use those circumstances and wounds to help us to grow and change, then we can surely be well and free. The damaging experiences will always be there in memory for they happened, in our reality. But memory can be put in its place, namely a ghost of the past from which to release and move on.

Insight

People sometimes notice how good it is to be still and rest, watching the sky go by, listening to the birds and feeling at peace inside, but first they need to take that first step and lie down.

The willingness to be well in itself can open up the opportunities for this to take place. It doesn't happen overnight but seeds have first to be planted in the heart. Nurturing and feeding has to be regular, growing begins gradually, blossoming is then inevitable.

Ask yourself, 'Do I allow fear to prevent me from doing the things I want to do?'

▶ *'Do I experience fear as a familiar feeling?'*
▶ *'Am I ever free of pain/suffering?'*
▶ *'Am I blessed to have love in my life?'*
▶ *'Do I really want to be well and live life in love and joy?'*
▶ *'If I were to be born again in this moment, what/who is it I would want to be in my life?'*

Insight

Find things to love about yourself and others. When your mind judges, take a look at what is good in your life. Look at the similarities in people rather than the differences, and have compassion in the faults you see in others as they are surely your own.

There is comfort in knowing that whatever you are feeling you are not alone. It is supposed to feel like this given your past, your personality, your circumstance, your attitude, your habits, your lack of love and, let's face it, your parents!

Love can be recreated by our interaction with nature and communication with other human beings. Love, respect and caring are natural reactions to open and honest communication. Intense personal love can be regenerated by the physical union through sexual union. Personal love is concentrated universal love. Sex by itself is a temporary release of energy. Sex in communion with love that is consciously expressed via the body to another creates the ultimate in giving and receiving of the senses. Divine love is only experienced in lovemaking when each partner is fully alert in the present, leaves behind their obsession with sex and addiction to fantasy, and is one hundred per cent faithful in thought as well as deed. Fantasy creates phantoms to which most people give their attention during sex.

Divine physical union occurs when sexual excitement is replaced with the surrender to love by both partners simultaneously with neither one becoming unconscious for even a second. Divine passion is carried on the breath, so breath awareness allows for the bliss to traverse the energy fields, merging them into one. Once this has been experienced you will never want or even need sex again. Making love is fully satisfying and ceases to be an obsessive hunt for the passing moment again. All senses are sharpened. To gain this experience, Reiki self-treatment to the genitals, in private, together with the heart position, will lessen the excitement and increase the feeling of complete bliss throughout the body.

Sex obsession or dissatisfaction comes about through a disconnection with the root chakra at the base of the spine and the heart. When all energy centres are aligned and healthy, sex is no longer possible, only sexual love is possible. It is a rare person who will admit their dissatisfaction with the endless repetition of their discontent.

Sexuality is a dynamic creative force. It permeates every level of life. When out of balance with our sexuality and our identity on the scale of male/female, masculine/feminine it becomes a painful issue that cannot seem to be resolved. There is so much guilt and blame instilled in us about sex from an early age. We are hung up if we enjoy it, if we don't enjoy it, if we like it or don't like it, if we do it or don't do it. The most fundamental force of life becomes the most taboo subject as those who should, or could, teach us are hesitant to pass on their own discontent and misunderstanding. It is often not until we find out what we don't want that we find what we do want. Trial and error causes devastating pain and suffering and irreparable damage to our hearts.

Divine Love can only be truly experienced through the heart, for within the heart lie the seeds of joy and contentment, of longing and fulfilment, of thirst and that thirst being quenched. To accept sex without love is to deny yourself happiness in truth. Have none of it.

Inside the heart lies the treasure that we all seek, the knowledge of all knowledge, the answer that has no question. Indeed, in the place of the heart the quest is ended. Although the physical heart is in the body, universal heart is in the soul. The bliss is felt when the soul unites with the spirit again through the sensory magnificence of the body.

One quality of love is to give love, the other is to receive love. Both allow the love to remain in motion throughout humanity. Self-love through the heart leads to self-worth, not egotism. We also need colour, taste, smell, music, sound, speed, communication, feeling and dreams.

Reiki practice brings one to attention and focus with the intention for healing to occur. Through physical posture – the form – breath awareness is made, the mind settles and becomes controlled. The session enforces rest without sleep, in the presence of another, and may bring about clear sleep when needed. Dreams become more colourful yet less fearful. Spiritual knowledge is gained through awakening the inner light. We move towards fresher more colourful food and pure water, we long to have fresh air and walk in the sun. As we begin to love our own self we attract loving relationships that nurture. Purpose is fulfilled.

The solution is within the human heart.

Listening Hands exercise – barefoot stillwalking

Stand in the garden, barefoot, feet shoulder-width apart, knees unlocked and eyes open. Look at the plants growing. Look every day at how they change. From a still point, walk very slowly and very quietly in a relaxed manner. Allow the breath to be itself. Become slower still, to the point where if you were to go any slower you would begin to become unbalanced. Keep to the point of balance. Keep walking round. When you are calm and the mind begins to quieten, continue with the following. As the breath comes in, lift the first foot to walk. It should reach level with the other leg as the breath turns from in to out. As the foot continues forward it is on the breath out. Keep moving until the weight is on the front foot at the end of the out breath. As the breath turns again, lift the other foot and continue in this manner. The walk now follows the breath. As you begin to relax, the breath begins to slow and lengthen, thus slowing and lengthening the step. After 10 to 15 minutes of this exercise you will feel that the rush of living has left you. Shake out the hands and the feet.

10 THINGS TO REMEMBER

1   You can only breathe one breath at a time – one breath in, one breath out.

2   Exercise assimilates all substances into useful energy.

3   Water is vital. It allows for vibrant energetic messages to pass through the body.

4   The food on your plate is the body of tomorrow.

5   By feeding your body consciously, you are nurturing your soul.

6   Rest gives access to stored energy.

7   Let go of habits and addictions that keep you in a state of unhappiness.

8   Dreaming while asleep releases the subconscious. Dreaming while awake creates possible futures.

9   Music brings joy as you can only listen in the present.

10   To receive love is great, to give love is even better.

7

Initiation

In this chapter you will learn:

- *the essence of Reiki, what actually takes place during the one-to-one transmission of energy that makes Reiki different from other forms of healing*
- *to realize the possibility of awakening the Divine Light for self-knowledge*
- *an exercise in releasing tension within the body to create physical relaxation.*

Every idea that becomes an ideal engenders life force within you.

Rudolph Steiner

Insight

Go and try everything else and if you don't find what you are looking for, please come back and I will show you the missing piece.

The transference of divine knowledge is not to do with intellect or even on the level of mind. It is to do with the communicating of force fields, one feeding from the other without stealing. Physical presence is therefore necessary. A book can give the theory, information, technique and guidelines but the teacher's presence is needed for the transmission to be complete. It is not that this particular teacher is any more special than the student, it is that the teacher has received the gift themselves and become apprentice to nurturing its growth. They have passed through the transmission process many times themselves and understand the sacred purity of energy that does not come from personality. In this respect it is vital to receive the initiations from a teacher who has a strong groundwork in the knowledge of Being through apprenticeship. Learning in one weekend to teach Reiki will not allow the student to receive the quality of transference they require or deserve. Value yourself, save up, travel, accept only the best.

Firstly the Master prepares in private with the 'Method for Activating Energy', which is fully described in Chapter 11 after Master's Level 1.

When the student is seated, prepared for initiation, they are willingly giving the Master permission to lift them up, to take their hand and show them the way. Dis-ease in the soul and mind structures prevents this awareness from being clear as a glimpse is only a glimpse, a possibility of what is available once the student has gone home and interacts in the life they have created from low energy. At home it is easy to forget. So effort in self-treatment is stressed. During self-treatment, if the effort is sincerely made, the place of pure consciousness can re-emerge. Gradually it becomes clearly understood until the point at which it remains. Once the energy/chakra system becomes balanced the maintenance of consciousness is one of devotion to the practice in order not to forget the still point.

The experiences of the heart are many and various, but when divine love is felt in a state of full awareness then the purpose of life is naturally and completely understood. A radiance can be seen at the completion of the initiations that was not seen before. It was always there but lying dormant, covered by the masks of anxiety, fear and hurt. The place of the heart is within. It is an experience that surpasses all others. It is one from which no one can separate you, nor can they steal.

When the students wake up to receive they see that the gift has already been given.

So, you see, Reiki cannot be bought, as it is already yours. That is not what the exchange is for. It is for the expenses, time, effort and dedication of the Master who is willing to hold your energy for you while you metamorphose into a wakeful consciousness. The exchange is given to open the gateway of willingness to receive.

Recently I was talking to a lady who was suffering severe back pain and stress due to endless wrong decisions. She said the pain was so bad that she would do anything to be free of it, absolutely anything. I suggested some treatment or maybe training. Next day she showed me the new magnetic bracelet she had bought, for the price of the training. 'I'm told it will take away the pain and help me to sleep', she said. For the first week I was impressed – then the pain returned. If she left the bracelet off the pain was unbearable.

Yes, I was impressed with the power of such a little device. It was certainly altering her magnetic field and changing her energy level, but what about the body's messages? We need to see the messages and return to the source in order to heal rather than suppress the symptoms, as drugs would do, in order not to deal with the issues at hand, i.e. the wrong decision making, and the stressful attitude. I personally prefer to rely on my own hands to realign my magnetic field and recharge my energy system. I would never risk losing my health for losing my bracelet. I want to know that the changes taking place in me are about growth and wholeness. I can only rely on the creative energy to alter my field and would 'do anything' to know that, live with that, be that.

The obsession in the world is for materialism, followed by spiritual materialism. It is having both feet in the wrong camp. Don't get me wrong, I love the world and its abundance of entertainment and beautiful things – I wouldn't be without my hoard of collected, colourful but useless (and mainly broken) objects. But I would give up everything I own to have an experience of being in my heart. From that place nothing else is needed.

Reiki is not only the transmission of energy but also the transference of knowledge. Not information, but the knowledge – knowledge of the heart, knowledge of the creator. The transmission is done by invocation, but the transference is made by the Master's own knowledge of the Divine and by their ability to be directly connected to the Reiki within them as the initiation takes place. Another reason to choose wisely in your teacher.

Preparation of the Master is as essential as the student. The technique for transmission is simple and easy to learn. It involves the Usui symbols to call forth and activate the various levels of consciousness to which they pertain. They are keys to unlock energy of a particular vibration that is utilized in a specific way, enabling the Reiki to be accessed, unhindered by the personality of the giver. The Master needs to prepare by returning to the state of creative consciousness available only through dedication and devotional practice. The Master may appear to be sitting still and at times doing nothing, but in the doing nothing a vast field of energy is being held for you to contact. At the point of teaching, the Master must have more energy than the student in order to lift them up into the experience of Divine Knowledge. Just giving information of a technique does not suffice.

It is very common for the student in their dis-ease to be in a state of poverty consciousness, not just financial – some use that as an excuse not to come – but also emotional, mental, spiritual, undeserving and unworthiness. 'Why should the world give me anything when I can't do anything for myself?' 'Why should I give anything to the world when the world doesn't give me anything?' Long-term discontent will do this. So, as the student sits in the chair in order to receive their first initiation, I remind myself what a big step this is for them.

Chakras

I have used a variety of Chinese, Japanese and Indian words within the text describing methods and parts of the energy system. These words have been chosen as they are the ones we, in the West, are most familiar with and have incorporated into our vocabulary when there has been an inadequacy in our own

(Contd)

First we need to understand the energy body and the pathway through which Reiki will flow (see page 85). The body has seven major centres of concentrated energy that are called Chakras – an Indian word meaning wheel. The Chakras are vortexes that spin and vibrate over specific areas of the body to maintain its form and homeostasis. The Chakras are located as follows:

1 *'The Root' – at the base of the spine.*
   This centre is our contact with the outside density of the world. It is the place where harmony is established with the Natural Law of survival, linking to the tribal mind.
2 *'The Sacral' – at the navel or Hara.*
   This centre is our connection with creativity, vitality, stability, empathy with others and partnership.
3 *'The Solar Plexus' – in the centre of the thorax below the ribs.*
   This centre is the power house for Divine Will, choices, psychic and physical energy, learning and Truth.
4 *'The Heart' – in the centre of the chest.*
   This Chakra is the seat of unconditional love, harmony between the manifest and unmanifest worlds. The central

centre containing purpose, fulfillment and the possibility of eternal bliss.

5 'The Throat' – at the throat.
This centre is our essential point of communication with others. The voice of Divine made manifest. Where we express individuality.

6 'The Brow' or 'The Third Eye' – in the centre of the forehead. This centre gives insight, spiritual understanding, vision, clarity and encompasses the whole view – totality.

7 'The Crown' – at the fontanelle on top of the head. It is called the crown as that is how it appears to those who can see it; it also relates to the divine connection, the crown of creation. This centre gives an expansion of consciousness and unites us with a divine experience, that of pure being (Further descriptions of the Chakras are given in Chapter 8 during the application of self-treatment.)

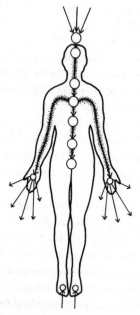

Figure 7.1 Reiki's pathway through the Chakras.

These are natural healing centres of the body that already exist. They function as an integrated circuit changing one form of energy into another. There are many other Chakras of smaller size and speed located all over the body following a map of fine energy lines called meridians. There are strong Chakras located in the centre of the soles of the feet – where connection to the Earth's energy is made for rooting and receiving – and the centre of the palms of the hand – where connection to the World is made for manifesting and giving. The main Chakras should be neither opened nor closed during transmission, as this can be a dangerous process, but they are realigned in such a way that the energy access is made available and does not revert to its original form. The Chakras are affected by external electromagnetic fields as well as the fields of other beings. Interference from these fields creates a breakdown in electrical communication between systems. After the initiation alignment, the Chakras become more integrated and self-regulatory, therefore we become generally less vulnerable to weakness.

The initiations are the essential part of the Form, the difference between Reiki and all other forms of healing. They allow the pathway of energy to be drawn down through the top of the head, through the heart, into the solar plexus and out through the hands. They alter the vibrational flow of the body and align it in such a way as to gain permanent access to the source of all things. I use the analogy of a hose pipe turned on but with a kink in it. The Master has been trained to find the kink and undo it so the water can flow freely once again. It is really nothing new, only a remembering.

For thousands of years the energy vortexes have been looked at for diagnosis and healing in all forms of energy medicine. They are an essential part of the structure of metaphysical science. They are like the skeleton of the energy body. This body exudes an electromagnetic force field that can be detected. Many people can see the Chakras and the force field, or aura as it is called, as either a hazy mirage, moving lights or transparent waves of colour. Many more who cannot see them can detect them with their hands. This energy body occupies the same space at the same time as the physical body yet is less dense and more expanded. The aura is an interconnecting web of fields rather than a set of layers and is seen as being egg-shaped in a healthy individual. There is a theory that two things cannot occupy the same space at the same time – the physical is a mere manifestation of its energy body vibrating in a dance with the external world. The energy vortexes are a bridge between the unseen and the seen, an interface between the subtle and the physical worlds.

Each of the seven main centres form the endocrine system in the physical body – the system of hormone regulators, the emotional signals, experiences of well-being and Being.

Through correctly practised meditation, it is possible to alter the spin of the centres to 'open' them. This can be a very dangerous practice unless you are guided by an adept. The Chakras open naturally when there is knowledge, understanding and awakened consciousness.

Entrainment

During attunement, a change takes place within the student by a scientific process known as 'entrainment'. Entrainment is when two oscillating electromagnetic systems come into each other's proximity, each operating at its own frequency, or vibration. Both frequencies change resonation to become synchronized with the other, the lower lifting towards the higher. In this way, the energy that emanates from the Master at the time of initiation engages the energy of the student in the process of that entrainment. This electromagnetic resonance settles at the higher frequency that is most natural to it, which is why we feel better. This is also found to be the dominant process during the treatment. The energy of the practitioner aligns with that of the receiver, the two pulse as one, the energy of the receiver raises itself by following the resonance. The advanced Reiki techniques give the practitioner tools to activate the electromagnetism in the hands and the ability to be more conscious of this experience. Even the breath can become naturally co-ordinated and as one is breathing out, the other is breathing in. This assists the balance and unity and creates the clarity needed for the healing to take place.

> **Insight**
>
> When resonating a tuning fork, other tuning forks nearby will vibrate with the same sound even if they have not been struck. This describes entrainment. In this way, when the client begins to quieten and relax in the process of a Reiki treatment, they are captured by entrainment. The electromagnetic energy field of the practitioner aligns, as one, with that of the client. After the treatment the client will feel changed in a profound way.

The form of First Degree initiation

During the initiation the student agrees to receive and the Master is in a state to give. The exchange is made to create the gateway for return. There are four initiations for First Degree. The first aligns the crown, the second the heart, the third the solar plexus and the fourth seals the pathway through the hands. From the first session the energy begins to flow. Many people ask what happens during the initiation as we ask them to close their eyes.

The initiations begin with the student seated and the Master behind in preparation. The Master first makes conscious contact with the pure Reiki and focuses the intent. The Master bows, in gratitude, to the Reiki Masters in their lineage as a sign of respect for the gift; they bow to the student as a sign of service and respect for the student. The first invocation begins over the crown to call upon the energy to align in this way. Several of the sacred symbols are used at this point to unlock the energy vibration. With one hand over the crown a silent invocation is made to call upon the Divine White Light to enter. Once this is activated the hand is placed on the head and the invocation continues. The Master then comes to the front of the student and clasps their hands in a posture for the invocation of Divine Light to come through the hands. The hands are lifted above the brow and a Holy Breath is formed to blow a cleansing breath on the hands, brow and crown. A Holy Breath is given to the heart and solar plexus also.

The hand clasp is sealed with a further invocation as the energy begins to enter the hands. The Master passes behind the student again and, using an empowerment posture and gesture with the hands, blesses the student and bows in gratitude. A clap brings the student into the present.

The second and third initiations follow the above pattern and include invocation via the hands of the Master on the shoulders of the student, energizing the throat and heart chakras. The fourth initiation follows the same path as the first but after the crown has been energized, the Master's hands gently cup the head as an invocation is made to seal the new experience.

The purpose of four sessions is a gradual alignment interspersed with grounding by practical experience, questioning and knowledge-giving sessions.

Sometimes nothing seems to be felt at all during this profound and powerful process and the student looks up in amazement with an 'Is that it?' question in their eyes. Other times, warmth and tingling can be felt. Some people have wonderful visions, or symbolic colours appear. Some like the place so much that they almost refuse to return, so I clap loudly at the end! Experience is as varied as the diversity of people. The initiations are performed one to one in silence. Sometimes the second, third and fourth can be undertaken in small groups but no more than three at a time. The Master must not interfere with the process with ego as may happen in a large group.

The moment of initiation brings about union with Reiki – union with the Divine – and needs respect. It is a ritual of invocation and direction of Divine Light, a holy act of purification. The initiation in itself will transform as it changes the essential vibrational frequency of the student. The frequency with which the soul-self of the student operates is raised so that what is put out is in balance and harmony, therefore what comes back in circumstance and relationship is also in balance and harmony.

Once the full initiation has taken place, this alignment remains eternally. It is possible, however, to focus on the mind, the emotions and the negativity of the world and thereby mask the openness to God. But it will still be there waiting for you to return with your effort and practice.

Experiences at initiation

Insight

Reiki takes you slowly and gently to a beautiful place inside where everything is at rest. Something begins to stir and awaken deep within. Gradually the heart feels a great warmth that was not there before and, in that moment, all becomes well with the world.

'At the first initiation the light in my head went glorious blue and in it "swam" an eagle bearing a gold bead in its beak; the eagle told me I was safe now and to follow it. The colour changed to gold flashing with white and blue. An eye appeared in the centre like an open flower.'

'I felt profound peace and calm as soon as the hand was on my head. I wanted it to stay there for ever.'

'At first everything went dark, I couldn't breathe, I was surely dying! Then a kaleidoscope of colours flashed before me. My hands tingled and felt they were being pushed apart. The heat was tremendous. I was not afraid.'

'I felt some buzzing in my arms, coming down from my head and back into my palms. The tips of my fingers wanted to dance.'

'At first I didn't feel a thing, but each initiation changed me in some way. During the second one, columns appeared, in the third a gypsy was standing at my side holding out a light to me in her hand, in the fourth I was in a fountain of exquisite beauty: it was washing me and my pain into such a happy place.'

'Nothing happened in the initiation, but when I came to move I was stuck. It became unbearably funny and we giggled for at least five minutes. A hug soon brought reality back, unfortunately.'

'I have been paralysed down one side of my face and one arm for 25 years due to a riding accident. From the first initiation energy began to move in me. I made a jump as a spider invaded my calm and crawled across my cheek. When I opened my eyes I realized there was no spider, it was my hair brushing the face that I hadn't felt in 25 years. I was so shocked and stunned that I had to lie down and have a cup of tea!'

'I went into initiation with a splitting headache, I wasn't sure this was the right time to be doing all this but had paid what I felt to be a lot of money and come a long way so thought I wouldn't say anything. You know, I don't like to make a fuss! When the Master blew on my head it felt like cool soothing rain, the pain in my head split into pieces and followed the rain. I remained very still and quiet. I dared not move in case the beautiful feeling was not real. It remained with me all day. During the next initiation nothing at all happened but I knew something would never be the same again.'

'It felt like mumbo-jumbo to me, but the main thing was, my friend had been helped so much with the Reiki that I continued. I have to admit I felt a lot of moving and energy during the treatment practice so the mumbo-jumbo aspect slipped into the background. For me, seeing is believing.'

'When the initiation began, a pile of grief and hopelessness welled up in me and came pouring out of my eyes. I was not exactly crying as my breath was normal but the feelings of sadness rose and rose and tears poured out of me. Sandi did not seem put off by my inability to be composed and carried on. After the blowing, I felt like pieces of paper were floating off me and on each one was written my sorrows. Sandi held my shoulders at the end for a good five minutes until I felt better. I loved the course. It was a turning point that changed my life. I felt the veils lift off and what I needed to do to repair my sad life became clear.'

There is no doubt in my mind that Reiki changes lives.

Make preparation no more for the guest has arrived. Go and welcome him.

Maharaji

Listening Hands exercise – releasing tension

Sit or lie quietly somewhere. Begin with the toes. Imagine a piece of rope tied in a knot around your toes ... imagine reaching out and carefully untying the knot, releasing it and letting go. Move to your ankles ... imagine a knot tied inside your ankles, a knot of tension; imagine untying the knot, release it and let go. Move up to the calves ... imagine a knot inside the calves, untie the knot, release it and let it go. Move up to the knees ... imagine a knot in the knees, untie the knot, release it and let it go. Move to the hips ... imagine a knot in each hip, untie the knot slowly, release it and let it go. Move into the centre of the pelvis ... imagine a large knot of strong rope inside you, holding on to your tensions. As you carefully untie the knot you may begin to notice how expanded that place begins to feel. Move to the solar plexus ... imagine a knot tied deep within the solar plexus, tied tight through years of fear; untie the knot, release it and let go. Move to the heart in the centre of the chest ... imagine a strong knot, holding in your hurt and pain; untie the knot, release it and let it go. Move to the shoulder muscles ... imagine a knot on each side, a heavy knot that has become a burden to you; untie the knot and let it go.

Move to the hands ... imagine a knot in each hand, tied tight to restrict what you can do; untie that knot, release it and let it go. Move to the face ... imagine a rope full of knots that makes up the tension in your face, the hurt, the tears, the hiding; untie the knots one by one and let them go. Feel freedom. Move to the inside of the head, the brain ... imagine a large knot preventing your brain from functioning freely, preventing positive thoughts, preventing energy from awakening; untie the knot carefully and let go. Feel the freedom, the space in your body, the lightness now that all the burdens and tensions have been released. You did that.

10 THINGS TO REMEMBER

1   *Anyone can learn Reiki. But each experience of it is personal.*

2   *The Reiki attunements are unique. They are what make Reiki different from other forms of healing.*

3   *The transmission of energy is also the transference of knowledge.*

4   *The symbols are keys that unlock aspects of consciousness.*

5   *The attunement allows Reiki to flow freely regardless of the ability of the person.*

6   *The Chakras realign themselves when there is knowledge, understanding and awakened consciousness. There is no need to interfere with them.*

7   *White light contains all the other colours.*

8   *The moment of initiation brings about a union with Reiki and a reunion with the Self.*

9   *The attunement is a ritual in which Divine Light is invoked.*

10 *Metamorphosis takes place while you are busy doing something else.*

8

First Degree Reiki part one:
self-treatment

In this chapter you will learn:
- *about the processes and practical postures to focus healing on oneself, and a way to consolidate the changes in a safe and focused way*
- *a simple form to follow that gives confidence in practice*
- *the importance of self-treatment as a way to relax yet shift the energy within yourself*
- *an exercise in meditation to pull away from the chaos of everyday life to find a still point within.*

She had no edges, no outline, she flowed out and merged with table, chair, open door, sunlight.

Michele Roberts, *Impossible Saints*

Treating yourself

Insight

In Japanese, Reiki Level 1 is known as 'Shoden', Reiki Level 2 is 'Okuden' and Master Level is 'Shinpiden'.

It must be stressed that self-treatment is the most important aspect of Reiki. To treat others allows us to give and feel a sense of purpose, but to be able to address our own pain, suffering and difficulties is self-empowering. It is not until we refer back to our own attitude with a view to change that we can look out compassionately to the world of others.

Decide how much time to put aside for self-treatment. Half an hour a day is recommended for a steady and comfortable transformation to take place, but to begin with it is whatever you will allow yourself. Many people find that before bedtime or first thing in the morning are the easiest times to put aside. Self-treatment is best performed lying down as the arms are held by gravity and don't ache as they do when practised sitting upright.

Insight

People sometimes think they will have to give things up before they can aquire the gift of healing, but nothing is required of them other than openness and willingness to look in the direction that the finger of the Master is pointing.

The initiation must first be undertaken and energy exchanged for the transmission of awareness to begin to flow.

Find a quiet place where you will not be disturbed. Turn off the telephone, put out the cat and be sure your children are occupied. Treat this time as precious – the time you have always been waiting for among the noise, the hustle and bustle, the demands and stresses of the day. It is best not to play relaxing music as this will only entertain the mind and distract it from entering deep within.

Lie down with feet uncrossed and begin with a couple of minutes Re-Lax Breath (see page 6) to bring the awareness to the present. Remind yourself that for this session the worries and tensions are not needed. Let the hands become Listening Hands. Keep the fingers relaxed yet together so that the hand and fingers act as one complete unit.

As you place the hands on each position, all that is required is that you firstly observe the mind chatter and secondly, allow it to quieten. It is also best to allow the body to settle into each position for a minute first so that the implantation is on a deep and subtle level. Use of the visualization words is explained on page 110.

THE FORM OF SELF-TREATMENT

When you are ready, begin.

Position 1: Place the hands over the eyes

This position takes the sense of sight inwards, quietening the mind and allowing the energy to be drawn in to all parts of the physical eye, the sinuses and sense of smell, the head and even through to the far reaches of the body. It slows down the outward projection of the soul, allowing stillness and inward exploration to begin. It eventually awakens the Third Eye, that is the place of spiritual insight, allowing the vision to clear and the understanding of energy in all things to become obvious. All the experiences following treatment are subtle but become understood more as you progress with your effort and practice.

This position relates to the Brow Chakra, the colour of which is violet or indigo/purple. The relative organ is the pituitary gland. The visualization and word association is Inner Light.

An experience of colours may occur as flashes, waves, raindrops or, a common experience, as a large pulsating 'eye' or 'sun'. Energy may be felt throughout the body as a pulse, a tingle or a flow. It is also common to feel absolutely nothing at all! This can be the most soothing of experiences as a lot of the time we are in stress, tension or general overactivity in the brain. This position may bring about the ability to see the colour of energy in motion. Seeing pure Reiki.

Position 2: Place the hands over the top of the head

The hands cup the head, containing both sides of the brain together. This helps to calm and quieten the mind and integrate the cells of the brain back to active balance. It is especially beneficial for combating stress, remembering and learning difficulties. All of us tend to overuse one side of the brain and this allows the qualities of the other to be made more readily available. The right side of the brain governs the left body but also our creativity, intuition, visions, ideals, dreams and the experience of the transcendent and lateral impulses (artist, poet, musician, dancer, carer). The left side of the brain governs the right body but also our sense of logic, numbers, rational thinking, order, structure and focus (doctor, dentist, engineer, mathematician, bank manager). This position is good for anxiety, hyperactivity, worry, disconnection, and general balance of thought.

An experience of calm and peace may occur interspersed with further activity of the mind. The purity of Reiki as the great white light.

This position relates to the Crown Chakra, the colour of which is white or gold. The relative organ is the pineal gland. The visualization and word association is Sun.

Position 3: Place the hands around the jaw including the jaw muscle

The muscles of the jaw are very strong and hold on tight to unexpressed anger. Problems in the back teeth often occur after a period of unexpressed or even expressed anger as the residue is clenched in and reinforced in the night through dreams and tooth grinding. To sort out your dentistry you must also sort out your anger. This position feels very soothing, like 'being held in the mother's arms'.

By focusing on the comfort of this position and bringing the awareness into the back of the throat it is possible to experience pure bliss. It has also been noted that a sweet flavour can be detected that does not relate to any food in our diet. The Sages call this the flavour of the Absolute. The substance produced bathes the subtle body with love. That is why this position feels so primordial and comforting. The flavour of Reiki.

The visualization and word associations are Soma or Nectar.

Position 4: The hands tuck underneath the head

This is a very supportive position, and is particularly effective for combating exhaustion, anxiety, headache and mental tension. For severe migraine place one hand under the head and one on the forehead, but continue to do full body treatment as the cause of headaches is rarely in the head. Energy can begin to flow down the neck, releasing the muscles and allowing the nerves to function more fully.

Experience of colour may occur here also, although the quality of colour will be different from that on the brow. There is a further quietening of the mind and the beginning of a plunging deep into a quiet and still place.

This position relates to the Alter Major Chakra, the colour of which is brown. The relative organ is the sinuses. The visualization and word association is Moon.

Position 5: Cup the ears

By placing the hands over the ears we take the sense of sound inwards and stop the projection of soul into the world. Reiki has been found to reduce tinnitus and even repair nerve damage that causes deafness. It is a great pain reliever for children's ear infections. This position enhances the inner awareness of quiet and calm. It is the area that governs our physical, mental and emotional balance.

We often relax by entertaining the ears on the outside, projecting our hearing onto the radio, television or music – all fine in their place, yet we are missing out on the profound experience of stillness and silence. It is said by the Rishis, Sages and many modern-day Gurus that the journey on the Sound Current is the highest vehicle for enlightenment. Half an hour per day focusing on this position alone would bring about great physiological change and an enlightened consciousness. Don't neglect your whole body self-treatment, however!

The sound current is the easiest form of energy to identify. It begins with just a hissing in the ears yet, as we focus, it begins to expand laterally into many layers of sound, rumbles, whistles, bells and instruments. It is known as celestial music, music of the cosmos or the sound of the spheres. In outer space, where there are vast expanses of emptiness, this music has been recorded as the pure sound of quantum energy in motion. The sounds of the planets as they spin, the sound of our body as it lives, the sound of one hand clapping! Listening to Reiki in motion as it comes into being.

Not only can the subtle sounds be heard when we practise this position, but gradually an underlying level of hearing is revealed that had not before been heard. We begin to hear what people are not saying and start to understand our bodily energy experiences as related to the truth in the word of others. Of course, we must also wake up to the truth in the word of ourselves and begin to live it. It is what the Native Americans call 'to walk your talk'. Living in truth takes honourable commitment.

The visualization and word association is Sound (as this is a very powerful technique, the ultimate mantras can only be revealed through initiation from an adept).

Position 6: Place the hands over the throat

The throat is the area of communication, how we express ourselves. It is often noticed that when people receive Reiki treatment their voice becomes slightly deeper and clearer. The words used to speak contain more power. This is because when under pressure in a small tight energy field the voice is pushed up into the throat, the tone becomes unsure, whiny and negative words are used. When the Reiki has been given, the energy field expands, allowing the voice to expand down into the chest and abdomen. A well-projected and honest voice comes from the Hara, or navel, not the throat. Openness of word follows openness of energy. This position also covers the vocal chords and many glands in the neck such as the lymph nodes, tonsils and thyroid gland, the thyroid being the hormonal seat of metabolism, how we assimilate our nourishment and at what speed.

Not only do people experience a change in voice tone but also an ability to communicate better through more assertion and less aggression.

This position relates to the Throat Chakra the colour of which is blue. The relative organ is the thyroid gland. The visualization and word association is Harmony.

Position 7: The heart and solar plexus

Place one hand on the heart and the other on the solar plexus.
This is the position we naturally adopt when in deep fear, shock
or emotional distress. So by placing the hands here we can
calm our emotions, dispel all fears and strengthen our heart
in trust.

....

Insight

Find things to love about yourself and others. When your
mind judges, take a look at what is good in your life. Look at
the similarities in people rather than the differences, and have
compassion in the faults you see in others as they are surely
your own.

....

The heart is the seat of love. Without it we could not exist.
Without love, or the promise of love, we would fade and die, but
through addressing Reiki to this place only fear and pain die.
This is the seat of unconditional love – the love we may have for
our children and family, the love we may have for nature, and
the love we may have for life itself. Sometimes through deep hurt
we learn to condition ourselves into gaining conditional love.
Our personalities are forced to gain constant approval of others
and we live in the fear that if we don't come up to scratch then
love will be taken away from us. The only gift greater than being
loved is that of being able to love. Lucky is the one who has both
and is grateful. Reiki on the heart produces the experience of
unconditional love as love for life itself.

The hand on the heart allows it to warm, soften and open which, in time, creates the ability to stand and face the world 'square on'. If our emotions are holding us down then to heal this area can lift us up. Likewise, if it seems that it is someone else's attitude holding us down then we can lift ourselves up and become strong enough to make new choices.

Reiki on the solar plexus helps to calm the adrenalin-fed emotions by releasing the diaphragm wherein lie the blocks associated with agony, ecstasy, fear, fight/flight, grief, sorrow, loss of love, jealousy, greed, obsession, passion and control. It brings about a strengthening of the intuition, will power, personality, self-esteem, self-respect and a sense of trust. The solar plexus is the area where we not only digest and assimilate our physical food but are also fed subtle signals from the outside world. It is a vortex-like drum which feels every vibration in the atmosphere. If we are balanced and well the energy received can be assimilated, filtered and utilized to nourish the body/mind/soul. If we are out of balance then the energy received may be misinterpreted, harmful and stored in the physical organs, creating a blockage of the Chi and ultimately the implosion of energy that causes illness. Practising the positions of the heart and solar plexus together is very powerful.

(If you have particular trouble in the areas of liver (anger) or spleen (inertia), you can add this position: one hand just below the ribs of one side and the opposite hand holding the opposite shoulder muscle like a hug. Change and do the same for the other side.) We also become aware of the breath in the stillness of this position. When conscious of the breath the contact with the Divine remains unbroken. We naturally breathe in harmony with nature which in turn is in harmony with the Divine Laws. The breath divides individual personal life from Divine Life. Becoming conscious of the spaces between the in and the out breath unites the two.

The heart/solar plexus position relates firstly to the Heart Chakra, the colour of which is green. The relative organ is the thymus. The visualization and word association is Grace.

This position also relates to the Solar Plexus Chakra, the colour of which is yellow. The relative organ is the pancreas. The visualization and word association is Intuition.

Position 8: The lower abdomen

Place the hands in a V-shape on the lower abdomen. This position is very comforting and usually generates some warmth. It is very useful for any digestive disorders, constipation, diarrhoea, irritable bowel syndrome, allergies, food intolerance and the subtle art of holding on and letting go on the emotional level. For women it is of great comfort during periods, pre-menstrual tension and menopausal symptoms. Regular Reiki self-treatment has helped many couples who find fertility and conception difficult. Several of my own clients have become pregnant within a few months of treatment or learning when previously it had not happened. It has also been found helpful in cases of repeated miscarriage. Self-treatment seems to give the extra energy needed to continue to full term. As Reiki can do no harm, it is totally safe for use during pregnancy.

This position brings about great relief from pain due to digestive, eliminatory or reproductive causes.

This position relates to the Sacral Chakra, the colour of which is orange. The relative organ is the gonads. The visualization and word association is Hara.

Position 9: The genitals

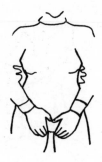

This area contains the powerful force of sexuality and procreation. Many of us have a big issue about our sexuality whether through obsession, fantasy or fear. Much confusion and distress are stored here as it is the area relating to the outside physical world. When treated with respect, true sexual union feeds the divine body only when love is present and fantasy ceases, otherwise there is always a need for more as the space is never filled. Divine healing takes place on the level of relationship.

Any physical problems are due either to a blockage of energy or over-activity. When we are out of balance we lose our instinct, sense of belonging, true nature and the security of our roots. This results in materialism, obsessive sexual fantasy and preoccupation with finding ourselves 'out there'. Balanced sexual union creates light in every cell; imbalanced union creates only our perpetual discontent. Of course, once in balance it is up to us what we do with it!

This position relates to the Root Chakra, the colour of which is red. The relative organs are the adrenals. The visualization and word association is Transcendence.

Position 10: The knees

If you have not yet fallen asleep, the leg positions are best done seated. Place one hand at the back and one on the top of one knee. Repeat on the other knee.

This position helps bring energy through the legs and unblocks Chi in the joints. Many people suffer from knee injury due to too much sport during the fast growth spurt of puberty.

The visualization and word association is I am flexible as I move forward.

Position 11: The ankles and feet

Place one hand on the ankle and one on the sole of the foot, then change to the other side. This is a remarkably pleasant feeling. The ankles take much strain and often create blocks in the Chi that prevent us from 'earthing' or 'grounding'. The energy lines (called meridians in Chinese medicine) pass through the ankles and into the toes, therefore by addressing energy to the feet we can, in effect, create an energy access to all other parts of the body. By allowing the Chi to earth through the feet we no longer overload (and no longer suffer from cold feet!). It is similar to the electrical system of your house: without the earthing wire, you are always on the verge of electrocution and overload! Our bodies are no different. The high water content together with metal elements in the blood and cells create the perfect live wire.

The visualization and word association is I return to Earth.

* * * * *

Reiki treatment is like relaxing in a warm and fragrant bath when you wish to slow down. Reiki Finishing-off Technique is like having an invigorating shower. If you are in bed at night then just go to sleep after the treatment above, remembering to give thanks to the Reiki by bringing your arms to cross over the chest and saying silently, 'Thank you for this healing, thank you for this healing, thank you for this healing'.

If you are practising in the morning or need to energize and wake yourself up, then continue through the all-important finishing.

Self-treatment – the finishing-off technique

The purpose of this part of the form is to give the deeply relaxed body a sense of its boundary once more and to stimulate the surface body to awaken without the sense of deep relaxation being taken away.

1 *Rotate the ankle both ways to its limit.*
2 *Massage the toes and foot deeply with the thumbs.*
3 *With both hands, squeeze up the leg three times from the ankle to the hip.*
4 *Again with both hands, stroke the leg in an energetic upward motion and sweep off at the top. This follow-through with the Chi is very important to produce an effect to the surface body. It is the same with golf or tennis: hitting the ball is one thing, the follow-through will give the power needed for the full potential of energy to be utilized.*
5 *Repeat with the other leg.*
6 *Massage the hand.*
7 *Squeeze up the arm including the shoulder muscle.*
8 *Flick up the arm, as before, three times.*
9 *Repeat with the other hand.*
10 *'Gallop' the fingers in a tapping motion on the skull to enliven the brain.*
11 *Massage the ears, holding the lobes at the end.*
12 *Tap the centre of the chest three times to wake up the immune system.*
13 *Cross the hands over the chest to give thanks (see page 146, Giving thanks position).*
14 *Rest for a few minutes before getting up. Notice how expanded you feel.*

This technique is very useful by itself in times of stress, tiredness, lethargy, depression and grief as well as before exams, tests, interviews and long-distance driving. As emotions are stored in every cell, the act of the squeeze and the flick stimulate the tissue to release tensions and toxins. The eliminatory system wakes up and begins to purify the system. Note how much more alive and tingly you feel at the end of this part of the treatment.

So I stress again the importance of daily self-treatment as being the key to permanent strength and well-being.

Practise this simple method daily for three to six months before attempting to go further. An advanced technique for self-treatment is the repetition of the visualization word at the appropriate posture. Each visualization and word association may be said silently in the place of stillness. So, place the hands on, allow a quietening, relax, say the word as given at the end of each position instruction, let go. The purpose of this technique is to affirm at the appropriate place the true meaning and purpose of that area of the body. It regenerates the balanced function of that place in accordance with the Natural Law. Make it simple, don't comment on Why? and What? just say the word and let go. This technique becomes automatic in a short time, allowing this aspect of being to affect you in the place of transcendence (deep stillness within). This has been formulated from ancient teaching tried and tested over centuries and is unique.

Insight

Write a list of your strengths, then a list of your weaknesses. Your strengths are your backbone. They are yours alone and will not change or leave you. Your weaknesses, however, are temporary and only last as long as you set limitations on yourself. Weaknesses can be transformed into more strength, but it may take some effort.

Reiki and common ailments

A full treatment daily is the best recommendation for all ailments. If there is a recurring problem, however, then more attention can be placed on specific areas, but remember that where the symptom manifests may not necessarily be where the cause originates.

Many of the following will be familiar either to you personally or in someone you know. Many are referred to in Chapter 13 on Experiences with Reiki. This list comes from my experience in treatment practice and all have been presented as problems at some time. I marvel at the difference Reiki can make. If you suffer from any of these then your quality of life and enjoyment will be impaired.

- *headache*
- *back pain*
- *digestive disorders including Irritable Bowel Syndrome and food intolerance*
- *eye strain*
- *period pain and PMT*
- *muscular tension*
- *arthritis*
- *respiratory problems – asthma, persistent cough, etc.*
- *injury including broken bones and healing of wounds*
- *high or low blood pressure*
- *stress/distress and related conditions*
- *exhaustion*
- *insomnia*
- *depression*
- *bereavement and loss*
- *death and dying*
- *anger*
- *anxiety*
- *panic attacks*
- *phobias*
- *Obsessive Compulsive Disorder*
- *loss of libido and other sexual dysfunction*
- *eating disorders*
- *addiction or substance abuse*
- *giving up smoking*
- *helping with weight loss*
- *low self-esteem*
- *side effects of medication*
- *post-operative care and rehabilitation*
- *relationship difficulties – partner/parents/children/at work*

▶ *improved communication*
▶ *finding personal direction*

I will analyse the three main problems to give some idea as to the complexity of any condition.

Back pain

SYMPTOMS OF BACK PAIN

▶ *Dull ache*
▶ *Acute pain*
▶ *Pain worse on lying down or relaxing*
▶ *Burning sensation*
▶ *Inability to move; inability to keep still*
▶ *Tingling in the arms*
▶ *Numbness in the legs or soles of the feet*
▶ *Unintentional weight loss*
▶ *Knotted muscle spasm*
▶ *Anxiety*
▶ *Insomnia*
▶ *Shallow or laboured breathing*
▶ *Lower back pain extending down the leg (sciatica)*
▶ *Stoop/round shoulders/twist or crooked spine*
▶ *Slipped disc*
▶ *Pain on walking/sitting*
▶ *Continuous frown*

COMMON CAUSES OF BACK PAIN

▶ *Poor posture*
▶ *Muscle strain/weakness*
▶ *Sitting for a long time in a poor position (office desk)*
▶ *Lifting heavy object(s)*
▶ *Accident*
▶ *Post-operative recovery*

- *Poor diet and nutrition*
- *Inactivity*
- *Hereditary disease*
- *Age-related spinal degeneration and general weakness*
- *Smoking*
- *Coughing*
- *Kidney/urinary infection*
- *Emotional tension*
- *Unresolved grief*
- *Dark secrets*
- *Depression*
- *Cancer*

REMEDIES FOR HEALING AND PREVENTING BACK PAIN

- *Standard Reiki self-treatment programme*
- *Specific Reiki postures for condition (see later)*
- *Reassess lifestyle and use of spine*
- *Physiotherapy and medical supervision – specific exercise programme to strengthen muscles around spine to prevent further injury*
- *Walking for general fitness and fresh air*
- *Core strengthening – Pilates, yoga, Tai Chi*
- *Attention to nutrition – more fresh, less processed food – vitamin D from exposure to sunlight*
- *Rest and relaxation*
- *Sit upright, especially at a computer or when watching television, taking regular breaks to stretch or walk*
- *Sort out emotional problems*

SPECIFIC REIKI POSTURES FOR THE CONDITION

- *Both hands lower back*
- *Both hands mid-back (kidneys)*
- *One hand on lower back with other at back of neck*
- *Right hand on left shoulder muscle deeply massaging first then keeping still, left hand on right lower rib (like a hug, this helps*

*keep the hands in place without strain) change sides. Lying
down with pillow under the knees, place one hand on heart
and one on solar plexus. This can also release back muscles.*

Headache

Nearly everyone has experienced a headache. It is the kind of
pain that calls for immediate action as it prevents us from thinking,
functioning or even interacting successfully. Occasional headaches
can often be traced to a cause either in the environment, in the
diet or in the current levels of stress and responsibility. Constant,
severe or reoccurring headache may have a deeper underlying
origin and should therefore be assessed by your doctor. If you
routinely carry headache tablets then reassess your lifestyle and
focus on rebalancing yourself with a daily Reiki routine.

SYMPTOMS OF HEADACHE

- *Dull ache all over the head*
- *Severe throbbing*
- *Pain in the back of the head*
- *Pain over or in the eyes*
- *Pain over or in one eye*
- *Tight band across the forehead*
- *High temperature*
- *Nausea*
- *Indigestion*
- *Flashing lights*
- *Tunnel or distorted vision*
- *Dizziness*
- *Blindness*

COMMON CAUSES OF HEADACHE

- *Tension*
- *Lack of fresh air*

- Chemical smell
- Poor, neon or flashing lights
- Computer screen
- Night driving
- Eye strain
- Physical posture
- Emotional stress
- Anxiety/worry
- Food intolerance
- Temperature/virus/infection
- Glaucoma
- Sinus congestion
- Injury/fracture
- Migraine
- Stroke
- Cancer
- Tumour

REMEDIES FOR HEALING AND PREVENTING HEADACHE

- Reiki standard self-treatment programme
- Specific Reiki postures for this condition
- All Reiki positions that quieten the mind and calm emotions
- Relaxation techniques
- Head, neck and shoulder massage
- Just sitting, doing nothing
- Stillness, silence and darkness
- Pay attention to your diet and nutrition, avoiding over-indulgence, alcohol and coffee
- Change of lighting
- Fresh air
- Have an eye test to check vision and pressure
- Reduce stress levels
- Resolve emotional issues
- Breathe more fully
- Tai chi, yoga, exercise in fresh air
- Humming to release tension

SPECIFIC REIKI POSTURES FOR THIS CONDITION

- *Hands over the eyes for at least five minutes*
- *Be aware of relaxing the breath*
- *One hand on base of the skull (over the ridge at the back) with the other over the forehead*
- *Both hands wrap around to cover the neck at the back*
- *Heart and Solar plexus*
- *Massage the feet, especially the toes*

Digestive disorders

Many people suffer from discomfort and even embarrassment from digestive disorder. There are many causes of this condition, yet the solution is often as simple as eating more slowly and more consciously, making time for both cooking and meal times, and eating at the table rather than on the run or in front of the television. Look at the quality of the food on your plate and eat it with calm emotion, for your emotional attitude will affect both the digestion and the assimilation of food. Emotional distress can cause bowel dysfunction.

SYMPTOMS OF DIGESTIVE DISORDER

- *Irritable Bowel Syndrome*
- *Diarrhoea*
- *Constipation*
- *Indigestion*
- *Abdominal tension*
- *Cramps*
- *Wind*
- *Colitis*
- *Gurgling*
- *Incontinence*

- ▶ *Bleeding*
- ▶ *Nausea and vomiting*
- ▶ *Reflux*
- ▶ *Pain*
- ▶ *Tender liver*
- ▶ *Tender kidneys*
- ▶ *Tender bowel*
- ▶ *Embarrassment*

COMMON CAUSES OF DIGESTIVE DISORDER

- ▶ *Poor diet/limited food choices/allergy/ intolerance*
- ▶ *Lack of exercise*
- ▶ *Obesity*
- ▶ *Smoking*
- ▶ *Polyps/fissures/parasites*
- ▶ *Cancer ulcers*
- ▶ *Refined carbohydrates*
- ▶ *Sugar*
- ▶ *Caffeine*
- ▶ *Processed food*
- ▶ *Fat*
- ▶ *Lack of fibre*
- ▶ *Dehydration*
- ▶ *Dental problems*
- ▶ *Emotional tension*
- ▶ *Anxiety*
- ▶ *Disgust with body function*
- ▶ *Sexual dysfunction*
- ▶ *Secretive behaviour*
- ▶ *Drug/alcohol abuse*
- ▶ *Eating disorder*
- ▶ *Depression*
- ▶ *Energy depletion illness*
- ▶ *Side effects of medication*

REMEDIES FOR HEALING AND PREVENTING DIGESTIVE DISORDERS

▶ *Standard Reiki self-treatment programme*
▶ *Specific Reiki postures for condition*
▶ *Exercise – brisk walking, swimming*
▶ *Drinking more water*
▶ *Attention to diet (see Chapter 7)*
▶ *Eat more fibre-rich food*
▶ *Regular meals*
▶ *Relaxation techniques*
▶ *Relaxed breathing*
▶ *Mineral supplement*
▶ *Core strengthening – Pilates, yoga, Tai Chi*
▶ *Emotional therapy*
▶ *Test for allergy and food intolerance (commonly dairy and wheat)*
▶ *Massage lower abdomen from right to left in circles to encourage proper bowel movement*

SPECIFIC REIKI POSTURES FOR THE CONDITION

▶ *Left hand on spleen area (just below the left ribs), right hand on the liver area (just below the right ribs)*
▶ *Both hands across the waist at the back*
▶ *Both hands on the lower abdomen*
▶ *One hand on the heart and one on the solar plexus*
▶ *Finish off with a strong overall self-massage to stimulate circulation*

Questions and answers

Q *After I learn self-healing will I be able to give up my medication?*

A Your doctor is responsible for your diagnosis and medication so it is recommended that you consult with him/her if and when you feel ready to reduce it. Reiki brings about such changes that medication can frequently be reduced with supervision.

The reduction of symptoms and the regaining of energy will be an indication that change is taking place. Once you are off medication, Reiki self-treatment can keep your energy at a level of total well-being and prevent further decline.

Q *During treatment I started to cry for no apparent reason. Does this mean Reiki is not suitable for me?*

A Reiki is working very well here. Emotions locked in the body release during treatment without the need to know what their content is. Crying is a natural process of purification. Continue with the treatment and when you have finished you can start to look into what the emotion may be about.

Q *I have toothache quite often, will Reiki help me?*

A Reiki can considerably ease the pain of toothache but ultimately dental treatment will be needed. Once the gums and teeth are cleaned then Reiki can be used for preventive measures. Diet and oral hygiene should be looked into.

Q *My brother has MS. What could Reiki do for him?*

A Firstly, it may help ease his discomfort and bring about freedom of movement. Treatment is very supportive when someone has a serious degenerative illness as they frequently feel isolated and lonely. Learning Reiki would be good for your brother as he would be able to treat himself, which is of great comfort when becoming more and more dependent on others. Maybe someone close to him could also learn and give him regular treatments.

By drinking nectar one becomes immortal.

Unknown

Insight

One doesn't have to have any prior knowledge of the body, or illness or health in order to be able to take in the experience of Reiki. No note taking is necessary, just a willingness to relax and open to the possibility to feel something new.

Listening Hands exercise – meditation at the bottom of the ocean

Begin by sitting somewhere quiet and undisturbed. Sit on a cushion with your legs crossed if you can so that your spine remains erect throughout, do not lean against anything, rest your hands upturned in your lap. Relax and watch your breath for a little while to quieten the mind. Keeping your attention on your breath going slowly in and slowly out, imagine you are sitting at the bottom of the ocean on the sand ... you can breathe in water as if it was air ... you notice the long weeds flowing around you, growing long and tall up towards the light that seems to come from above ... the seaweed is swaying with the water ... it is all one ... you notice that you are swaying slightly, just naturally ... you feel like you are the weed ... you hear sounds like children playing on the beach but they are way above you out of the ocean ... no one knows you are here ... it is so still and peaceful, so supportive ... your mind chatters on from time to time but you realize that it is turning into beautiful coloured fish that swim away in little shoals ... some of your mind chatter bobbing up on the surface, floating on the waves like leaves or petals and is washed away to join the other noises way up on the sandy shore in the sun above ... down here you are alone at last ... all you have is the comfort of your breath as it goes quietly in, turns, and comes quietly out again. Stay with that feeling, stay with the sensation that the sun is safely above you somewhere but that here is somewhere where you can rest, where no one can find you, where life is eternal. Remain in this awareness for around 20 minutes. Slowly allow yourself to float up to the surface, swim to the shore and climb onto the beach where your friends are all playing. Come back to the room in the present, open your eyes but keep them downcast for a couple of minutes, then stretch and wake up.

10 THINGS TO REMEMBER

1 *Self-treatment can be practised on a daily basis.*

2 *A short version can be done, but cutting time will cut effect.*

3 *The hand positions cover the seven main Chakras.*

4 *Focus on the feeling.*

5 *Use the time wisely. Quieten the mind first, then the emotions and the body will follow.*

6 *Agitation in the mind will cause tension in the body. Tension in the body will cause agitation in the mind.*

7 *Look at all aspects of your self if you want to bring about good health.*

8 *Use the treatment to bring calm and the finishing-off technique to raise released energy.*

9 *Quench your thirst for love and happiness by giving Reiki to yourself.*

10 *Self-treatment improves the quality of the relationship with yourself.*

First Degree Reiki part two: treatment of others

In this chapter you will learn:

- *about the process and postures that enable you to treat family, friends and even pets*
- *the technique that forms the basis for both simple practice at home and professional therapy practice*
- *the hand positions that create a simple form to follow to support learning*
- *an exercise of the breath to awaken Divine Connection.*

When the student is ready the teacher will appear.

> **Insight**
>
> Visit The Stillpoint School of Reiki website
> www.teachyourselfreiki.co.uk for information about classes.
> Be willing to travel and see this as a special kind of holiday
> in which your spirit will be renewed. You will return home
> refreshed with this amazingly useful healing skill.

Reiki in practice – the Listening Hands technique

The learning environment must support the aspect of purity and simplicity first and foremost with nothing added from other disciplines. No New Age music, no gongs or chants, no clearing of stuff. It must contain only Reiki if anyone is to know what they are receiving. It must not be diluted with other ideas or dogmas, crystals, rattles or drums. These have a sacred place also but they are not appropriate here. It is for the Master, the Reiki and the student alone, for the student can experience what Reiki is only when they quieten the clutter of the mind and go within.

It is a unique way of learning. Most classes are taught with notebooks and pens. They are structured and much information is given out to be re-read at a later date as revision and reminders. Reiki is not learnt with the mind, it is a full experience and therefore cannot be forgotten. The initiations implant the connection within you like putting up a radio aerial and tuning it in to a particular frequency.

Insight

A subtle shift of awareness is produced and is enhanced by every treatment. Sooner or later comes the sense of taking back the power into your own hands, together with a renewed ability to cope and respond to life in a clear, balanced way.

A class is usually set out in four sessions with one initiation at the beginning of each session to allow the alignment to be gradual, with a practical grounding session in between. Generally anyone who is more than 12 weeks' pregnant will be asked to return for the initiations in about a year, as once the foetus is fully formed it is felt that it is being initiated also but without personal permission. It is, however, totally safe to learn, give and receive Reiki during pregnancy. It can greatly relieve the side-effects such as nausea and backache, and is wonderful during labour to replenish energy levels between contractions and prevent trauma.

It is important for the initiating Master to be aware of any medication being taken, especially if the student is undergoing, or has undergone in the past, treatment for depression or mental illness or suffers from any phobia or eating disorder. Drug and alcohol dependents will be given treatments rather than training until such time as they can begin the changes to be well. They are not ruled out but caution must be respected. Reiki sensitizes some people and care must be taken of them.

It must be noted that Reiki cannot be used for negative intent such as black magic or power over others as it always brings light and balance into being. Darkness cannot be empowered by light.

The energy exchange is made as people prepare to enter the first initiation. Once initiated, the energy begins to come through. All four First Degree initiations are necessary for the transmission to be complete. These may be condensed but nothing must be left out.

The ideal position in which to treat others is for them to lie down, fully clothed, with the shoes removed. This way they can reach a deep state of relaxation. Some people like to talk throughout a treatment in order not to face their fears but for most, eyes closed, in quietness, is best. Talking does not detract from the power of the Reiki but will detract from your experience of it.

It is possible to treat the whole body in a seated position which may be more appropriate for some elderly, pregnant, handicapped or disabled people or those who are sceptical and need gentle introduction. It must also be remembered that many people have fears about being touched. They may have deep-seated sexual issues or have suffered abuse. So, whatever is the most comfortable for the client will create the best results. For practitioners and those with Second Degree it is necessary to take a short case history, but for all others it is enough to ask about the structure of the body, for example, do they suffer any back pain, in order to help them be comfortable. If this is the case, a pillow under the knees will take strain off the lower back and one under the head will ease neck discomfort.

For the comfort and respect of the receiver, the practitioner should wash their hands before and after treatment. They should also clean their teeth and pay attention to personal hygiene. Strong perfumes should be avoided and garlic should not be eaten for up to 24 hours before a treatment. How can the receiver relax if the practitioner smells strongly? The positions keep both parties close and, although absolutely no intimate personal positions are used, it is still an intimate situation. The receiver may be apprehensive.

Firstly, stand and relax, tail tucked in, head up, knees unlocked, breath relaxed and gentle. You are there for the receiver. You are privileged to be witness and facilitator.

Use of the hands

Keep the attention/focus on the interface between your own hand and the body of the receiver; the place where the two meet is neither one nor the other. Be aware of the weight of your hands.

- *Do they cause pressure?*
- *Are they hovering and hesitant?*
- *Do they relax and support the body without interfering with it?*
- *Do they 'hold' the body with gentle yet confident respect?*
- *Does your attention waver from the interface to thoughts, causing the hands to change weight?*
- *Is this the most comfortable hold for the receiver? How does it feel to you?*
- *Are the hands placed in such a way as to be able to relax and put yourself aside?*
- *Does your hand placement interfere with the relaxation of your posture or your own breathing?*
- *Can you comfortably move from one position to another without the client noticing?*

The attention resides in the place where all that is felt is the varying sensations of energy in motion as you, literally, touch the light. It may not be clear yet as to whose energy you are feeling. Is it yours, is it theirs, is it from somewhere else? Just become a passive observer to the energy that may or may not have sensations of cold, heat, colour, tingling, fizzing, streaming, etc.

Keeping attention on the place of energy between the receiver and the hand prevents the energies from mingling or merging and thereby interfering with each other. It also gives the practitioner a focus away from the randomness of internal dialogue or indeed the ego-based commentary on experiences that may be seen as wonderfully psychic. The psychic field can develop quite rapidly with Reiki practice, especially at Second Degree and Masters Level 1, yet we must not concern ourselves with its over-importance as the purpose in hand is to see what it is doing for the receiver.

The bodies become open to each other for communication yet do not invade or affect each other directly from a level of personality. The Reiki is made accessible to the receiver via the conduit of the initiate who has, and maintains, through regular self-treatment, a clear pathway to the external reservoir of energy. The receiver's energy flow naturally draws from this reservoir down through the practitioner but does not take on any aspect of the practitioner's personality or personal energy imbalances. That would deplete the giver and be a form of energy stealing. The subconscious of the receiver knows, through its intrinsic creative intelligence, which parts of its integrative system need the attention of energy flow. Gradually the flow begins and sensations may occur as the moving field encounters places of stagnation, tension and blockage. The body has the ability to eliminate all substances that are detrimental to its well-being and will awaken its system of communication once the energy awakening commences.

Chronic illness has been caused and perpetuated over time, and it may take several treatments to begin to clear any density caused in the structure of the body. Chronic or traumatic illness creates changes in the skeletal structure also, as the energy blocks form substance in the eddies instead of freedom in the flow.

Insight
You may or may not notice the Reiki in your hands, but when the receiver tells you how warm and comforting it felt, then you know, without a doubt, that something special has taken place.

It has been seen that the energy centres create vortexes at intervals along the structure of the spine where the curvature turns away from centre. As the energy shifts direction, pressure builds up forming a spiral rhythm. This rhythm is the same as the one that originally sang within the foetus in morphic resonance as it formed each organ. Each endocrine organ is suspended at a plexus in the system corresponding to a change of direction of spinal flow.

It is good practice to correct the posture through techniques such as McTimoney Chiropractic, Alexander Technique, Hatha Yoga, Tai Chi, etc., to keep the spine healthy, flexible and strong with the correct curvature to sustain healthy Chakras and organ vibration. Our perpetual misuse of posture and shrinking is due to emotional displacement causing the Chakras and related organs to be placed under intense pressure. This eventually causes a number of serious conditions relating to hormone and metabolic imbalance.

It has been found that Reiki treatment can realign the spine, the pelvis and release traumatized muscles, tendons and ligaments. It can revitalize lesions, creating new pathways of energy to awaken nervous systems. No manipulation is necessary for this; just follow the simple non-invasive hands-on postures. Reiki allows the body to realign itself by giving it the opportunity and holding it there when it changes. Emotional trauma causes a physical trauma through the closing down of the various plexuses concerned.

Energy is neither given to a client nor taken away from a client. Removing negative blocks from someone else is a very dangerous thing to do. The energy they contain within them is in balance with their consciousness and must be allowed to grow at the same time. When negative energy is transformed by the light that Reiki is, then it becomes balanced. It is a misconception to think that negativity must be got rid of and positivity fed in. Leave the body alone to balance itself. It knows its own self a lot better than we can ever do consciously.

Holding someone still is the best that we can do. It is as important as simply listening when someone has a problem to voice, rather than offering solutions or changing the subject.

The mind needs to continue in its depth of study of whatever issues may arise during treatment. The content is of no importance to the practitioner and need not be exposed. The container is the person who is the vehicle for transforming the energy, by release, in the presence of another. This is a profound release, creating a deep repatterning of the soul. If we think we can interfere or manipulate the energy in some way to bring about a set outcome then we have missed the whole point. We are then, in effect, taking responsibility for the healing ourselves through our ego, and thereby dis-empowering the receiver. We are also open to thinking we know so much when the creative intelligence may have another journey for this individual. Leave the client alone, put yourself aside, relax, release any idea of doing anything. In the process of not doing is where the changes occur. Reiki does itself when given the chance. Remember to breathe and focus the intention.

The head and heart positions are the most important, but a whole body treatment is most beneficial to finding the root cause. It is not necessary to remove any clothing except shoes and glasses. The treatment is a very personal internal act and this aspect must be respected at all times, therefore no intimate positions are to be included and there is no invasion of privacy. It is possible to have very cold hands but for the receiver to experience burning heat, as what they feel is not body temperature but the transference of energy as it is drawn through.

Insight
All things are connected. Whatever befalls the Earth befalls the sons of the Earth. Man did not weave the web of life. He is merely a strand in it. Whatever he does to the web, he does to himself.

Chief Seattle

The form of treatment of others

THE HEAD AND HEART POSITIONS

The treatment begins with the preparation of the giver and a gentle introduction of the two bodies to gain a sense of confidence and trust. This is done with a non-invasive and gentle stroking of the forehead and hair, allowing the mind to begin to relax.

Each position over the major organs may be held for about two minutes. This allows the energy time to begin being drawn and the cells to release.

Firstly relax yourself, knees unlocked, tail tucked in, head free, and breathe. Focus on the fact that you are here for the receiver and are privileged to witness their growth.

Position 1

The hands are to make full contact with the body, avoiding pressure on the eyes. Keep the fingers together to form a complete unit of palm and fingers. The hands are placed gently and respectfully over the eyes with the thumbs down the middle of the forehead. Not too close to the nostrils. This position strengthens the Brow Chakra, the seat of the 'Third Eye', the spiritual seeing centre.

Position 2

The second position is over the head, either side of the brain. It is especially beneficial for combating stress and memory and learning difficulties. This position strengthens the Crown Chakra.

Position 3

The third position is around the jaw. It is soothing, like being 'held in the mother's arms'.

Position 4

The fourth position is with the hands cupped under the back of the head. This is a very supportive position, particularly effective for combating exhaustion, anxiety, headache and mental tension. This position strengthens the Alter Major.

Position 5

This is a simple cupping of the ears. This aids balance and listening to what is being said and what is not being said.

Position 6

The hands are crossed to form a V-shape that naturally fits over the throat. No pressure whatsoever must be put on the throat so the thumbs may rest lightly on the chin. This position strengthens the Throat Chakra.

Position 7

The hands join in a V-shape at the centre of the chest, being discreet with positions on women, especially if you are a man. It may be more appropriate to rest the thumbs on the collar bones and fan the hands out over the chest without contact. Some contact must be maintained as it will allow the person to stay deep within without rising up to the surface if the contact is discontinued. This position strengthens the Heart Chakra.

Position 8

The hands hold the soft part of the shoulder towards the arm, allowing energy to flow down the arms and into the lymph system in the armpits.

THE FRONT POSITIONS

Position 9

Working from the side now, the hands are placed side by side on the opposite side of the body on the lower ribs and liver/spleen.

Position 10

Slide the hands to the side nearest to you. Positions 9 and 10 energize the digestive and eliminatory system. They also strengthen the Solar Plexus Chakra. It is very common for the stomach and intestines to gurgle loudly as they kick into action and begin to move.

Position 11

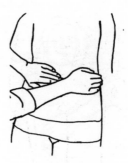

One hand is placed in front of the other across the lower waist/ navel; take care not to twist your back. This position strengthens the Sacral Chakra and assists the holding on and letting go in the bowels.

Position 12a

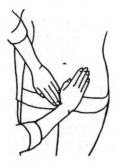

This position is different for men and for women as the giver must not become intimate with the receiver. Many people have deep issues over sexuality and you must never intrude on their intimate centres. The position for women is in a V-shape, as the woman would do on herself on the lower intestines. This covers all internal reproductive organs.

Position 12b

The position for men is with two hands, one in front of the other, resting on the bones of the top of the pelvis. Any problem in the lower internal area may be treated on the position on the lower back (see Position 21). This position relates to the Root Chakra.

Position 13

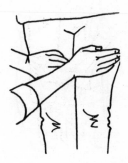

One hand is placed on each thigh. (This position and position 15, the shins, may be omitted if short of time but be sure to address the joints with Position 14, the knees, and Position 16, the ankles.)

Position 14

The hands move down to the knees. Change hands over as you move to prevent back strain.

Position 15

The shins.

Position 16

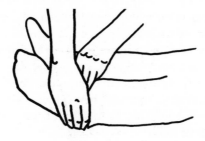

The ankles.

The feet are focused on at the end of the back positions as they are easier to hold when the receiver is lying on their front. Then the receiver is helped to turn over by firstly sitting up. The pillows are placed under the chest (if comfortable) and under the ankles.

THE BACK POSITIONS

It is common for emotion to arise during Reiki on the back positions as the vulnerable, openness of the front body is now covered. If emotion does arise it needs release, so lightly touch to the shoulder and quietly say a phrase such as, 'It's OK, it's a safe

place here, you can feel free to let go of anything uncomfortable.'
Continue the hand positions rather than entering into a counselling
session or a discussion of feelings at this stage. Let the receiver
reside in the turmoil with your protective hands holding them still.
Notice what is happening without comment, judgement or thinking
you should do anything with your observation. Take no credit for
the enjoyment or any blame or the seeming refusal of any pain to
shift. Reiki is the planting of the seed, a triggering of opportunity.
We cannot possibly know what the outcome will look like, we only
come to know through practice, dedication and experience that
this system is totally safe and can be trusted at all times to be the
catalyst for change.

As chaos is change in motion, any change in the energy body can
at first appear to have caused chaos, usually manifesting in the
emotional body. It is common to feel out of sorts for a while.
The chaos is order in the making but to the mind it appears out
of control. The mind must be subdued and surrendered to a still
place. Time must pass, more treatment made available. The more
chaotic the change seems, the quicker it shifts. I have seen people
a year after learning Reiki and not even recognized them as they
appear lighter, energetic, wear different coloured clothes and have
often changed their hair. They often appear contented and happy.
This is the power of Reiki.

Continue with the treatment down the back.

Position 17

Starting on the side farther away, one hand is placed high up on the shoulder muscle where much tension is stored and where we carry the burdens of life, the other is placed next to it covering the scapula or shoulder blade.

Position 18

The hands slide across the shoulders to the near side.

Position 19

One hand is placed in front of the other across the middle of the back. This is energizing the kidneys and allowing them to wake up and begin to eliminate more toxins.

Position 20

One hand is placed in front of the other across the waist. The back muscles support the whole torso.

Position 21

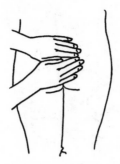

One hand is placed next to the other on the sacrum or lower spine. This allows deep release of structural tension in the pelvis due to misuse of posture, childbirth and ancestral blocks. The tensions in the lower back are mirrored in the neck. For obvious problems in both areas, place one hand on the neck and the other on the lower spine.

If there is a problem in the hips, such as arthritis or hip replacement, an additional position may be done here.

Position 22

One hand is placed on each of the upper thighs (again these may be omitted if lacking time).

Position 23

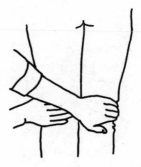

One hand is placed on the back of each knee.

Position 24

One hand is placed on each calf.

Position 25

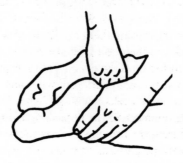

One hand is placed on each ankle.

Position 26

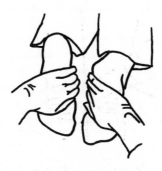

One hand is placed on each of the soles of the feet, with palms facing inwards. This is a very important position as it completes the process of energizing by awakening the meridians/energy lines that begin in the feet and connect through pathways in the body to various organs. It also allows the consciousness of the receiver to be earthed through the feet and for them to become completely 'at home' in the body.

These positions constitute the treatment. They are like being allowed to lie and rest in a warm bath. The finishing-off technique is an awakening, like having an invigorating shower, but is done slowly so that the receiver comes back into the boundaries of the body, if they may have floated off, and slowly returns to their centre and back into the room in the present moment. They may have been on a silent marathon journey inside and emerge profoundly changed. You do not want to disturb the feeling of relaxation but you must bring them to a state of wakefulness that is conscious and allows them to travel home safely, feeling good. You do not need to focus on the content of their journey unless they wish to do so as the assimilation of what has changed may take several days or even weeks to comprehend. It is a private and internal process. It often cannot be described. Pain and emotion may be released during the treatment in the form of crying and changes in the breathing patterns or it may be several days before the effects begin to show.

So, after the warm bath, the shower.

> **Insight**
>
> The heart speaks but only when we are able to listen to it.
> Listening can only happen when everything else around is
> still as the voice of the heart is very quiet. It will not shout at
> you, it will not bully you, it will not abandon you but it will
> patiently wait for you to be quiet and then you will find it
> whispering words of encouragement to you.

Treatment of others – the finishing-off technique

The technique is unique to this system and is a vital part of
the grounding process and integration of the energetic with the
physical.

1 *Lift one foot.*
2 *Rotate the ankle.*
3 *Put the foot down to give it a firm rub with the thumbs.
   Standing from the body side gives access for the thumbs to
   work down towards the toes and include the toes.*
4 *Using the whole hand, lay the palms on the leg and gently
   squeeze in to take up the slack. It is just the point where there
   begins to be a resistance. Continue up the leg in, maybe, three
   places. Repeat twice more, making three times altogether.*
5 *(See below.) Hold the ankle with the lower hand and with the
   soft, relaxed and loose palm of the other sweep up the surface
   of the leg, as if you were stroking hairs, or feeling the fabric,
   then continue to follow through with the sweep at the end. It
   is like playing tennis or golf. The energy, Chi or power comes
   from the follow-through. Do this three times upwards towards
   the heart. This enlivens the tissues, gives back the sense of
   boundary to the body and brings the energy into the centre.*

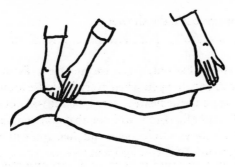

Figure 9.1 The finishing-off technique position 5.

6 Repeat with the other leg. If, owing to the weather being very hot, the receiver is wearing a skirt or little clothing it is best to place a blanket over their legs to do this.

7 Do the same with the arms. If there is a particular problem or injury in the arms then this is the place to address it. Hold the hand in your hand. Place the other hand for a few minutes on the centre of the back, then the shoulder, then the elbow and the wrist. Continue the finishing-off technique.
Release the wrist, massage the palm and fingers.
Standing beside the receiver, link your hand in theirs for support, squeeze up the arm and include the shoulder. This gives the person the sense of being reconnected with their body. Squeeze up the arms three times.

8 Stroke up the arm and flick off at the top with a follow-through sweep. Do this three times.

9 Repeat with the other arm.

10 (See below.) Stand beside the body and place one hand at the top of the spine. With the other hand sweep down either side of the spine three times, but not directly on it. This should be done very gently and should not cause any shaking in the body. It is literally like stroking hairs.

Figure 9.2 The finishing-off technique position 10.

11 *Rub the back in a circular motion and finish with one hand
    over the heart centre and one on the lower spine to give the
    body the message to remain calm, relaxed and still. Do not
    'stroke the aura' or 'fluff it up' as this interferes with the
    natural balance that is settling into place. The aura must
    remain calm and still and will change of its own accord when
    the body becomes balanced.*

12 *(See Giving thanks position, below.) Take one hand off and then
    the other, to avoid the feeling of abandonment in the receiver.
    Cross them across your chest or put them together and give
    thanks to Reiki. Say three times, 'Thank you for this healing'.
    Then quietly, with a hand on the receiver's shoulders say, 'The
    treatment is now finished, you can get up when you are ready.'*

Figure 9.3 Giving thanks position.

Help the person up from the bed or bench, and rub their shoulders
gently but vigorously to bring them back if they are still a bit
floaty. Offer water to drink.

This whole treatment should take from an hour to an hour and a half.

Insight

After a Reiki treatment a subtle shift of awareness is produced and is enhanced by each treatment. Sooner or later comes the sense of taking back power into your own hands, together with a renewed ability to cope and respond to life in a clear, balanced way.

Treating children

Figure 9.4 Giving Reiki to a child.

When treating children it is best to reduce the positions to include three on the head, then one on the heart, the tummy and finally, the feet. Children can be still for about 20 minutes at the most unless they are especially relaxed or ill. For my own children I put on their favourite story tape and practise some positions sitting next to them. For little children the Reiki can be given in the process of a long hug, or if they are ill, wait until they are asleep.

Children learn Reiki very easily. I would never teach anyone under the age of seven and always obtain permission from their parent first. The general rule is that one of the parents needs to have learnt first. I have one girl who learnt at nine who followed through the whole weekend with enthusiasm. She has a special gift and wanted to learn Reiki almost more than the rest of the family. A children's class is sometimes arranged which consists of energy activities as well as treatment, short form treatment, and meditation with Reiki.

> **Insight**
>
> Become childlike and lose some of those stuffy inhibitions. What gives pleasure to a child? Jumping in puddles, running down a hill and then doing it again and again just for the fun of it. Try running down a hill so fast that you actually feel out of control. Climb a tree, play leap-frog, laugh out loud – especially at yourself.

The cleansing process

There may be a cleansing of the system for several days after a treatment in the form of either loose bowels, feeling nauseous, headache or feeling very deflated, even flu-like symptoms may occur as the toxins are eliminated and the new frequency of energy adjusts in the physiology. Mostly, however, people feel relaxed and alert. They may comment on how clear colours are and the edges of objects. Their inner strength may quickly return. Always encourage an early night and the drinking of water after a treatment.

The 'healing crisis'

The healing crisis sometimes occurs. The cleansing process may be categorized as this but more extreme symptoms may occur, namely the worsening of the current illness before it gets better. Sometimes, on the rare occasion, a headache may occur, or nausea, or rash or even a temperature. This is not a sign that things have actually become worse but that the symptoms are moving to the surface and clearing out. This will pass in a few days. The habit of suppression of symptoms with medication may push an illness into a chronic deep state, the result of which is great discomfort as the body returns to balance. In this situation it is good to encourage the person to sit it out, drink water, rest and return for more treatment. Often, after the crisis has subsided, the person finds that their doctor is able to reduce the medication and sometimes even stop it altogether. I liken the healing crisis to a spring clean. In order to spring clean your house, firstly you must create more chaos before new order can be made. Unwanted things are revealed and can be discarded.

A common experience of giving Reiki is the enjoyment by the practitioner, as we simultaneously receive the energy and are replenished.

Place your tears in a cup of water – where is your sorrow now?
Sri Nisargadatta Maharaj

Insight

Children see fairies and have invisible friends. They stop seeing them when they become adults. We need to wake up to the possibility that other parallel worlds exist simultaneously to ours. Perhaps one day we will get a little glimpse of a fairy, a sprite or a dragon if we believe enough that the myth is a form of reality and not just a 'make believe'.

Listening Hands exercise – cosmic breathing

As you sit quietly, notice the breath as it comes in and flows out. Imagine a point of light millions of miles above your head in a straight line. As the breath comes in see this light drawn down into the centre of your body, filling your every last cell with light. As the breath goes out, watch the light return to its source above you. In this way the breath becomes down and up rather than in and out. It is drawn from a Divine Source that feels a million miles away in space but is actually deep within.

10 THINGS TO REMEMBER

1 *Reiki is not learnt with the mind. It is a whole experience.*

2 *When light shines on darkness, the darkness disappears.*

3 *Reiki is felt at the interface between the hand and the body.*

4 *Energy is neither given nor taken away. It is simply made accessible.*

5 *Reiki is performed fully clothed and remains non-invasive throughout.*

6 *The hands are placed on another person in respectful, gentle non-invasive touch.*

7 *We notice what is happening but without commenting, judging or thinking.*

8 *Reiki plants the seed of change.*

9 *The practitioner finds the giving process as enjoyable as the receiving.*

10 *The finishing-off technique is essential for complete integration.*

10

Second Degree Reiki

In this chapter you will learn:
* *about the processes and postures to activate distant healing as a doorway to in-depth understanding of energy*
* *how to integrate with the global consciousness and see the power of symbols in the consciousness of man*
* *an exercise to create lightness of being.*

In-depth and distant healing

Second Degree is known as 'the practitioner level'. It is an essential training for anyone wishing to practise Reiki as a profession, although that is not what it was originally for. The prerequisite for Second Degree is at least three months' practice of First Degree on self and others. For those people who are learning Reiki solely for their own well-being, self-treatment is sufficient, but some appreciation and understanding of the power, depth and magnitude of the system is needed and can only come from the experience through practice. This level calls to an individual when they are ready for it. Reiki is the guide.

Second Degree also entails an initiation transmission, during which the three Usui symbols and mantras are given. This must be taken with a qualified, registered Master. The application of the symbols is also given at initiation. My personal undertaking as a Master of Usui Shiki Ryoho is to keep the teaching of Reiki sacred. I am unable to reveal the symbols here as they must be transmitted along with their energy essence at initiation. They can be found in books but will not unlock the Divine at the depth to which pure consciousness is activated. Beware of attempting self-initiation, as is suggested in some books, as it can unlock energies that you may not require. There is that fine line between spiritual awakening and true madness.

It is best to receive knowledge information, i.e. the symbols and their uses, some days before the initiation in order to learn and become familiar with them. This makes their application smoother and the understanding easier.

> **Insight**
> *Everyone who is successful must have dreamed of something.*
>
> Maricopa, Native American

Sacred symbols

Ancient societies had no written word. Their knowledge, tribal rule of conduct and Divine Connection was passed on in oral tradition through the transmission during ritual, myths, songs, stories, visual images and sacred symbols. In ancient Egypt, the written word was considered an holy act. The writing and carving of symbols in tombs were not merely for storytelling, mythology or historical documentation, but for empowerment of the energy of the Ka or spirit to make its transition from the earth plane to the afterlife. The symbols themselves were known to contain the activation of Sacred Energy. They were used as part of a complicated system of ritual to serve a purpose. The scribes themselves were considered high priests and, as such, were awarded the privilege of having their own tombs.

The word 'sacred' means holy, of a divine nature. This is not the same as 'secret', which means hidden. Sacred is unseen and only revealed when consciousness allows. Secrets cause negative human emotions. A sacred name has great spiritual potency. The Reiki symbols that Dr Usui transmitted at initiation contain great powers that unlock specific areas of consciousness to empower us with the ability to create stuff from non-stuff, whether that be healing the body, balancing relationships or giving empowerment to world situations.

The student is carefully prepared with knowledge before entering into transmission of these skills. As the symbols are holy and contain much power they must only be revealed at the appropriate time. They are not withheld from view to create a mystery but in order that the student follows the preparatory path to be ready with understanding in due course.

There are many symbols that we use in our daily lives without much thought for their power. Road signs prevent us from accident by reminding the subconscious of the learnt set rules. Without them the roads would be in chaos. They keep order and provide instruction as we speed on by.

Astrological symbols contain the energy of deity. Each symbol represents a constellation, a planet or an energy. The combination of symbols within each person's birth chart reveals the energy of that person, their personality, strengths, weaknesses, directions, goals, etc. Each one on its own has specific characteristics of power. In combination they create a complex organism with infinite intelligence.

The Christian cross is a very powerful symbol to any Christian. It contains the whole essence of the teaching, the history, the form, the dogma and its origin. When drawn in the air above our head it becomes a blessing that unlocks the potential within all of us to become Christ consciousness. It is a protection and a purification.

Symbols drawn on card and placed in a room can change the effects of geopathic stress. The commonest are the starburst, which cleanses emotions and frees blocked Chi; the arrowhead, which strengthens willpower and harmonizes physical and spiritual energy; and the roundel which produces serenity and improves relationships. It is believed that crop circles are symbols containing a message from other life forms or even the Earth itself.

The Reiki symbols have an equal power and in combination unlock levels of creative intelligence that are simply astonishing and yet astonishingly simple. Symbols are, literally, radiators of their own symbolism. They create a quantum leap on the level of expanding consciousness. The essential Truth begins to become more obvious and the choices at every turn become fewer. There is a further quickening of the frequency of the student's energy body which makes their responsibility for awakening imperative. Their Karma – the Law of Action and Reaction – speeds up, calling upon honesty, clarity, stamina and eternal vigilance.

There are three symbols for Second Degree. Along with each symbol is a mantra, which is the sound vibration of the symbol – its name. Within the name is contained the whole form of what it is and, by repeating the mantra with focused intent, the form comes into Being.

Wallace D Wattles describes the manifestations of stuff out of non-stuff beautifully in his book *The Science of Getting Rich* (with Dr J Powell). Firstly he describes the unmanifest – Universal Energy – ...

> *There is a thinking stuff from which all things are made, and which, in its original state, permeates, penetrates, and fills the interspace of the Universe.*

... then our potential to influence it by the focus and intent of our mind ...

> *A thought in Substance produces the thing that is imagined by that thought.*

... and further to the final manifestation ...

you can form things in your thoughts, and, by impressing your thoughts upon the Formless Substance, can cause the thing you think about to be created.

That just about sums up Second Degree. The empowerment of the unmanifest Universal Life Force, activated with intent and specific mind stuff – symbol and mantra – created into manifest Being. Magnificent! Now watch what you think!

Mantras have been used for centuries for healing and divine connection. The Indian Pandits chant sacred mantras from the Vedic texts in Sanskrit. The power of the sound is enough to invoke altered states in those who hear it. Also in India, healing mantras are whispered into the ear of the patient; the vibration of the specific sound brings about profound change in both the body and in the aspect of the mind. The mantras, too, are revealed only when sufficient preparation and knowledge groundwork has been given. An example of a mantra we use in everyday life is our name. When our name is spoken in a crowded room *we* respond rather than someone else. It is who we have become. Sometimes you can look at a person and easily guess their name.

Insight
Imagination is more powerful than the will. Picture yourself in the future as a healthy, happy, energetic person who has love and friendship, security and purpose (and 7 pounds thinner, of course!). By imagining, it is only a question of time before the image becomes a reality.

So, once our thought is focused we can activate it into being. This is where the three symbols come in. The first makes a bridge between us and the person or situation we wish to contact; the second contacts the mental and emotional vibrational level; the third activates the process, empowers it with motion in an ever-expanding direction. Energy moves in a spinning spiral, from unlimited potential – via thought – into being.

Life force + direction + activation = creation.
Energy + focus + intent = manifestation.

Uses of Second Degree Reiki

The most important area of focus is self-treatment. The second
is what underlies the global mind-set – human consciousness.
To treat our self is increasing consciousness of the whole.
In addressing human consciousness we are including our self.
For in essence we are it and it is we.

Second Degree Reiki can be used for:

1 *Empowering the First Degree hands-on to go deeper more quickly. This may not be appropriate for everyone. The body must be present for this.*
2 *Instances when the body is not present (distant healing).*
3 *Individual physical, mental, emotional and spiritual healing, including children and animals.*
4 *Group healing.*
5 *Species of animals.*
6 *Areas of the world – conflict, war, famine, children, refugees, etc.*
7 *Situations – such as driving tests, exams, interviews, moving house, etc.*
8 *Relationships – between yourself and another, or a group, or other people's relationships.*
9 *People who are dying.*
10 *People who have died.*
11 *Spirits – this is not an area to enter into unless absolutely necessary as spirit entities are powerful invisible forces. They are so devious that they can disguise themselves as guides. Watch out, steer clear. Rudolph Steiner said in his book Higher Worlds, 'Contacting spirits in the hope of contacting God is a mistaken practice'. Aim for the highest and bypass all mediators, including spirits, and tap into your own self-empowering inherent wisdom instead. By playing with spirits you give your power away and become weak.*

> *Ghosts in the attic can be transmuted with the activation of Reiki, but again attempt this only if you feel at ease, otherwise leave well alone, call in an expert or move house!*

12 *Plants and species of plants.*
13 *The sending of love to our family.*
14 *The enhancement of prayer.*
15 *Self-treatment.*

Second Degree initiation

As a sign of respect for the process, both the Master and the student remove their shoes. The student willingly sits and gives the exchange, consciously focusing on what has been given and what is to be received. The magnitude of the gift cannot be underestimated. To learn First and Second Degree in just one day will not release the sacredness of the gift. If you value your journey and your awakening then value your gift also. It costs less than a holiday, less than a car service, and less than a bad habit! Reiki remains with you for the rest of your life.

The Master asks two questions:

1 *Do you take full responsibility for your own well-being?*
2 *Are you prepared for personal transformation?*

If 'Yes' is the answer to both questions the initiation transmission continues. The Master bows with respect and gratitude to the line of Masters and to the student. They prepare themselves by connecting to the Reiki within and putting the personality aside for this time. The silent invocation begins over the crown of the head and is taken into the hands. One hand is held up to receive and one hand is opened flat. Into this hand are drawn in turn the three sacred symbols, the bridge, the activator, and the mental/emotional symbol. The student is blessed with 'Holy Breath' and energizing begins. The Master claps to bring the student back to the present and bows to complete.

The practice can then begin.

The Universe does our bidding, it always has, so we must be clear in our commands, with gratitude and humility rather than unworthiness. We must never be afraid of the power or intelligence of the Universal Creator who has spoken these words through the host lord Krishna: 'Even in your darkest hour I will not abandon you'. We are created from the very consciousness of the Creator itself so when we ask we shall be given, with Grace, but must be careful what we ask for.

The most important issue when practising distant healing is to remember that permission must always be obtained for physical healing. For if we, without permission, take away a person's pain or illness with our great gift, then that person may recreate other symptoms in order for them to wake up to their own imbalance. If we ask permission it gives that person the opportunity to participate in their well-being and wake up to the symbolism of symptom. The only exception to this rule is for blood relatives who have a close karmic link with us, yet even so we must respect their beliefs and not send body healing if this would be an imposition or create fear and scepticism. There are ways of addressing this which we shall see later.

The process

First we sit somewhere quiet and comfortable, away from the children and the cat, away from the telephone and other pressing commitments. We take a minute to focus. Re-Lax Breath is useful (see page 6). Firstly the connection is made with the person requiring healing who has given permission. As the name is our personal mantra this is used to make contact. It does not have to be said out loud as the mind impression is a dynamic force and will link to the Being of the person wherever they are. Every invocation is repeated three times: this is to address the two levels of duality and contact the place of oneness. Father, Son and Holy

Ghost, the two sides and the centre. The manifest, the unmanifest and the void.

CONNECTION

We call their name three times. The person hears on an energetic level. By mental intention a thread of energy is sent out to the receiver, finding its way by matching the vibration and mantra. The thread is pulled back within the practitioner's own field without depleting the receiver or the giver. The practitioner's field becomes a place of safety. The unity is available to the receiver like pranic food, or intravenous vitality!

THE BRIDGE IS CREATED

We call upon the first symbol to make a bridge between us and the person receiving. We call the mantra of the symbol three times and draw the symbol in the air once with the initiated hand. See the power of the priest as he draws the blessing of the cross above our heads.

ACTIVATION IS THEN APPLIED

We then call upon the activation symbol three times and draw it once to create the life force spin which moves energy in time and space. This process brings the essence of the receiver to us here in the present, so we can lay our hands on their invisible energy body. Out of this relationship manifests new messages. This symbol is not only the activator of energy but the creator of substance by its very nature. It works in a vortex, the densest part of which is matter itself.

HANDS ON – ACCESS TO HEALING

There are many ways to keep the focus of this process but the easiest way is to place the person within yourself. We let the right leg represent the front of the person and divide it into three parts – the knee is the face and head, the mid-thigh is the centre of the body, the upper thigh is the hips, legs and feet. Likewise the left leg is divided to represent the back of the head, the back of the body and the back of the hips, legs and feet.

Figure 10.1 Physical treatment at a distance.

Place both hands on the right knee as corresponds to the head position; remain for a minute and a half – watch and wait. Notice what sensations and changes occur in the interface between the palm and the leg. From the moment we call the name, all sensations, symptoms and images are symbolic of the receiver in some way. Don't get too attached to these, however, as the important quality is that the Reiki is received. What we feel and see as possible psychic perceptions is just a by-product. The hands are applied to the energy body which is directly linked to the unified field. The field of the practitioner expands to embrace that of the receiver.

We spend five minutes in this way on the front of the body and also the back of the body. When this is complete, we have accessed the energy field for that person via their own energetic and physical body.

THE DISPOSITION

We call upon the mental/emotional symbol three times and draw it once in the air. This locks it onto the level of mind, emotion and subjective individuality. We then activate this energy level by again calling upon the activation symbol three times and drawing it out once.

Figure 10.2 Mental/emotional treatment at a distance.

We now hold the hands up, palms facing out (see above) with the fingers close and forming one unit, like radar dishes. They not only provide the access for Reiki to be drawn through, but also allow information to be received as to the quality of energy of the person, and sometimes even clues as to what else may be needed for their total well-being.

We invoke openness in the receiver by calling upon the affirmation three times – 'Divine Order, Harmony and Openness'. This gives access to the Divine Consciousness which is in perfect harmony and openness to receive it into their Being and personality, mind and emotions, to create change. We do not impose our ideas, thoughts or beliefs on them in any way.

We remain still for about five minutes watching and waiting. The quality of this energy can vary tremendously from person to person according to the depth of their illness or depression. It is often in this stillness that we recognize that energy is the only basic reality in our world. Our vision and perception begin to change the more we practise and let go.

GRATITUDE

At completion of the process we cross the hands over as before with gratitude and thanks. This process is so simple. It takes

15 minutes to give a full body, mental and emotional level treatment to a person at a distance. By crossing over the hands and detaching from the treatment this sends the energetic body 'home' and separates us from the receiver, so that no residue is left within us and they remain complete also. This process is vital as it is protection from remaining merged. When the short session is over the practitioner breaks with the field and the thread, thereby sending it back home to the receiver with the change of Chi. The energy continues to draw in from the unified field even after the process is complete. The session acts as a catalyst for a new speed of function.

So to sum up:

- *Obtain permission.*
- *Call the name three times.*
- *Call the bridge mantra three times. Draw the symbol once.*
- *Call the activation mantra three times. Draw once.*
- *Hands on.*
- *Call the disposition mantra three times. Draw once.*
- *Call the activation mantra three times. Draw once.*
- *Access energy through the hands up.*
- *Call Divine Order, Harmony and Openness three times. Let go.*
- *Close with crossed hands and thanks.*

The full body treatment takes only five minutes for the front and five minutes for the back, during which time many signals, symbols and symptoms may be detected through our hands or in ourselves. It is possible to feel the full extent of the pain or emotion of the receiver in our own body, but this dissipates once we disconnect ourselves at the end with the process of giving gratitude. The essential body returns home to the physical body, taking with it any residue.

Being physically close to someone will not guarantee a merging of energy fields or connection. We may be more connected with someone miles away. This proves that it is the intention and direction of mind that links the field. When mutual agreement is given, as with the ethic of permission in distant healing, the fields expand and unite. One field affects another. We can treat the other as 'I am'.

Our psychic perception greatly increases as we focus, yet let go, but we must not get caught up in these perceptions as the form, as they are really only distractions from the purpose of the Form which is, namely, to give access to another for the Reiki to be drawn through. That is all. We can, in fact, put ourselves aside and enjoy the trust and stillness, the opportunity for us to meditate. It is tempting to desire to become masters of perception and call ourselves that mysterious name 'psychic'. Psychic really only means seeing clearly and in order to do that we must firstly let go of our attachment to materialism, to illness and pain and above all our attachment to being noticed as doing good. It is required that we wake up and stay vigilant, then all will be revealed.

So this simple routine is used for any single treatment at a distance to include the physical, with permission. When permission has not been obtained and we are therefore unable to address the physical, we can still send Divine Order, Harmony and Openness. I see it as a cloud of light that can be sent to be near the person who can draw upon it if they wish by the statement of openness. This can be used for situations also, such as world events, conflict, etc.

The form of this is as follows:

▸ *Call the name three times.*
▸ *Call the bridge mantra three times. Draw the symbol once.*
▸ *Call the activation mantra three times. Draw once.*
▸ *Miss out the hands-on section and go straight on to …*
▸ *Call the disposition mantra three times. Draw once.*
▸ *Call the activation mantra three times. Draw once.*
▸ *Access energy through the hands up.*
▸ *Call Divine Order, Harmony and Openness three times. Let go.*
▸ *Close with crossed hands and thanks.*

In this way we can do the best that we can without interfering in another person's choices or Karma. The form above is also what is used for all other processes such as relationships between people, job interviews, moving house, etc., as with all these things there is no body and therefore no hands on. To access the Reiki for a relationship between two people we begin by calling the situation three times, like the name. This can be worded 'The relationship between … and …', i.e. myself and my parents, Joe and Jane Bloggs. Then the pattern already described is followed in order to make Divine Order, Harmony and Openness available to them and for them to be open to receiving it.

The outcome of the process cannot be anticipated and we cannot manipulate the end result. We must remember as we give thanks that the Divine Will knows all things and sets in motion a perfect journey for each individual according to their learning needs. Sometimes this even means that their illness does not go away but their eyes may open to another aspect of life. We must let go of all attachment to the outcome and simply trust. Only then can we see the magic in the mundane.

So for all other issues the only concern is how to word it simply and concisely, remembering always to repeat this three times to begin the manifestation. Situation and relationship issues are usually about what has not yet happened. So to send balance and harmony to the current energy of the situation or relationship will alter the future outcome. This must never be done by manipulation or egotistical needs to have the future a certain way.

To access Reiki for children we follow the same pattern as in the first session, but include the hands on only if permission has been obtained from the parent or guardian. It is wise to talk to the child about it and ask their permission also. When we come to place the hands on we can use the knees as before or, if the child is a baby, we can project them out in front of us and place the hands on the image. This way needs more focus and concentration but we can change the size of the child and also rotate them to place the hands in easier positions. Always remember to begin with the head and heart, working down to hold the feet at the end. After covering the body this way, continue with the original process by calling upon the mental/emotional mantra and symbol, activating it and placing the hands up as before. Complete with giving thanks.

TREATING ANIMALS

This process of projection can also be used for animals. It is very useful when the animal is large, for example, a horse or a cow. We can reduce their size in the image and thereby cover the whole body. With animals, and I suppose it would be true of people, I find it is most effective to have someone give them a hands-on treatment while you, or even a few of you, give distant Reiki at the same time. This is very empowering. Domestic pets often suffer from emotional imbalances such as anxiety and depression. Think of the neurotic dog that paces rapidly up and down or becomes hyperactive and obsessional, also the cat who is thin, quiet and avoids everyone. They respond well to Reiki, especially to Second Degree where affirmations can be used.

Figure 10.3 Treating a dog hands on.

Treating a cat hands on.

Often, with pets, the owner must also be treated as they may be the source of the problem through ignorance of animal behaviour and their emotional or even physical needs. I once knew of a crocodile that was kept in a bath. He was very depressed and lethargic. He didn't need much Reiki, he just needed to have a proper stimulating environment where he could be himself. Follow the same principles as for people, beginning with the head and heart positions. Animals also have a well-developed Chakra at the end of the nose and the base of the tail, with a lesser one at the tip of the tail bone. Their Third Eye Chakra is also well developed. They usually take as much Reiki as they want and move on.

Self-healing with Second Degree Reiki

For healing oneself with Second Degree Reiki we follow exactly the same path. We call our own name three times and by creating the bridge we can activate our energetic self to switch outside of our self, briefly, into the knees so that we place our own hands on our own body. In this way we treat our self with much more care and kindness. We continue through the positions and during the 'Divine Order, Harmony and Openness' section we can create affirmations to implant within the depth of the psyche. We finish with giving thanks and return our self within our self. Self-treatment is about improving our relationship with our self and therefore the way we respond to the world around us.

Affirmations

> **Insight**
> Believe in yourself. Get motivated to increase your energy, be creative in your thinking and raise yourself up in health and satisfaction. Be content with less but still have an ambition to push for more. Not more stuff, but more time, pleasure and love.

Affirmations are the invocation of positive patterning. They must always be in the present tense, so 'you are well' not 'you will be well', as that is always in the future, and not a negative such as 'you will not be angry'. This focuses the person on (a) resistance and (b) anger; instead it must be 'you are calm'. Personally I always use the first person 'I' instead of 'you' as, when the connection is made, we become I for the duration of the treatment. To find the most suitable affirmation I ask my client, 'How do you feel?' If they say, 'I'm feeling out of control and very anxious' I then say, 'And how would you like to feel?' Their reply may be 'I want to feel calm and in control', in which case the affirmation would be, 'I feel calm and in control'. This would be repeated three times after Divine Order, Harmony and Openness. Then just let go, watch and wait. Give thanks. It is good to make a list of common negative emotions and their complementary affirmation and begin to create a new vocabulary for yourself.

- *I feel angry/I feel calm.*
- *I feel out of control/I am in control.*
- *I feel very depressed and suicidal/I am happy and enjoy life.*
- *I am afraid of what might happen/I look forward to the future with confidence.*
- *I'm so stupid and ugly/What I am has beauty and strength.*
- *I don't know what to do/I make conscious decisions.*
- *There's no point/I am inspired and can choose my own future.*
- *It's all their fault, they did it to me/I take responsibility for my life and well-being.*
- *I'm so lonely/I am able to give with joy.*

This is just a sample. There are many books on affirmation; some are listed in the further reading section at the end of this book. To learn how to make effective affirmations for others, firstly begin by making a journal of your own and try them out. Very often we need affirmations, as our self-esteem has been destroyed by what we think others are thinking about us. It is good to begin to look at other people's needs instead of other people's thoughts. More often than not they are not thinking of us at all but of their own random internal dialogue. Sometimes we even make ourselves ill by worrying about what others think of us when we don't even really care or particularly like those people. So our own mind creates a trap of illusion with what it imagines. The way to remedy this is to stop for a moment and affirm something positive in the present tense and let others take care of their own heads and possible judgement of us. Only we know our own truth.

Another use of Second Degree is that of further empowering the hands-on treatment when a body is present. At the beginning of a normal body treatment we introduce the two bodies together and begin with the first position over the eyes. When this position has begun we can call the Second Degree into action in our mind's eye. I liken it to drawing your name in the air, in the dark, with a sparkler. Symbols and mantras must not be waved about all over the client as this creates a mystery and an element of fearful mumbo-jumbo. The mental/emotional mantra is silently repeated three times in the mind and drawn once with the sparkler, it is activated with the activation mantra and symbol, also silently in the mind, and then let go. This creates a boost in the energy access and also the depth to which it immediately reaches. Once set up this power remains throughout the treatment until the giving of thanks at the end. No more invocation is needed. The bridge is not needed as the body is already present. This process can also be applied during hands-on self-treatment, or the mental/emotional symbol and the activator symbol can be drawn on your own head before beginning the usual hands-on positions. The two symbols can be drawn on the side of the head before continuing with the treatment.

With the ability of Second Degree comes the ability to affect all levels of energy and therefore all living things and all energetic patterns such as situations, etc., that are still in the process of becoming. As all things are constantly in motion and change, this effect influences the motion of energy to become more in harmony with all the Laws of Nature that truly govern the Earth and her creatures. Man's manipulation of the Natural Laws has led him to become lost in his own quagmire. The only escape is to let go of the manipulation and power trip to come back to the inherent simplicity and trust that rewards us with joy of life and joy of living.

Group practice

Second Degree also allows each student to be a part of a network, if they wish, to heal as a group. The group becomes available for anyone requiring healing assistance for any reason. Each person remains in their own home and co-ordinates through a phone tree with the receiver or the organizer at a given time. This can be a group of any number. I personally use a network of between 12 and 20 for people or situations in crisis. It is not always necessary for all to 'send' at a specific time, but if the receiver is prepared and waiting it can be extremely powerful, especially in cases of serious illness, trauma and bereavement. The support felt by someone who is very ill in hospital by a group who they may not even know is tremendous.

My friend Trish died of cancer a few years ago. She was in a great state of anxiety towards the end, as everyone around her was trying to convince her she was going to be all right but she knew she was dying. The Reiki network became a deep support that she felt and appreciated right to the end. Her family were marvellous but, as with many families, communication was not always easy. She died just a few minutes after having a very peaceful Reiki treatment which finished with a long session to her heart. When our time is up let us be prepared by experiencing pure energy and being, the joy among the suffering.

There are group crisis lines for Reiki, national and international (see further information at the end of this book), as well as my own network should anyone require it for crisis, trauma, serious accident or illness, operations, situations, or friends and relatives. Group treatment is more than the power of the number of people.

Further group work can be carried out by a local support/sharing group. Three people constitute a group! So if one student wants to practise positions, receive Reiki or ask questions they can call up a couple of others and invite them round. My Second Degree students often like to do this and are usually better able to answer questions about energy as Second Degree dives one into a lateral view of the quantum field. For group work it is best for one person to lie down and the others to place their hands on the body as symmetrically as possible, keeping the hands light as it can be overwhelming. The heat generated can be wonderful. I once had a review class of 17 of my students, eight of whom also had Second Degree. It was midsummer's day, scorching hot sunshine. I lay on the bench in the garden and 34 hands were laid on me. I felt as if I had died and gone to heaven! It was like a world embrace that healed all my hurt child, my loneliness and my anger in one go. Please note, for a group this number is not recommended as it took us most of the day to get round everyone. Each person needs only about 15 minutes' group treatment as an equivalent to a one to one. Finishing-off is recommended to prevent the feeling of floating!

Second Degree Reiki can be used any time, any place, anywhere, for anyone and any situation. What more do you need? Practice, that's all. Practice to become familiar with the unseen, the unfamiliar. Practice to begin to know your true self and the workings of the Chi within. Practice to see the unity of yourself with all things as energy in motion. From nowhere, to somewhere, and to nowhere again.

Insight
Treat the Earth well. It was not given to you by your parents, it was loaned to you by your children.

Native American

Questions and answers

Q *I'm too strung up to lie still and don't have the time. I don't suppose I'd be calm enough to receive it. What do you think?*

A I'm sure you can find the time if you want to. You could have a shorter treatment of Second Degree, sitting in a chair, maybe listen to some music that you like. A little bit is better than none at all. Head and heart positions will help to start with. There is always a way to adapt to the individual's needs.

Q *I don't like being touched but I have had an operation that won't heal. What can I do?*

A Your therapist will be able to give you a treatment with hands off about two or three inches away from the body. You can sit in a chair if you are nervous about lying down. If you want to learn then you can just watch the group and practise self-treatment. It is possible to learn one to one, receive the initiations and just do self-treatment. No touching of or by others is necessary. Of course, the alternative is to receive distant Reiki.

Q *My husband says I shouldn't learn Reiki as it is not part of the Christian faith. Is this true?*

A Jesus did not call his healing Reiki, but when he placed his hands on people their energy changed and they were well. All life comes from the same source, but as humans we put that understanding into different forms and religions. We choose the one that is right for us but need not be blinkered to the potential of other things. Reiki is from the Creator direct. You can but try it and if you don't like it then don't do it. There is no obligation.

Contacting spirits in the hope of contacting God is mistaken practice.

Rudolph Steiner

Listening Hands exercise – the loop of light

Lie down in a quiet place. First thing in the morning is best for this exercise. Relax. Be aware of the boundaries of your body. Imagine your energy body the same shape and size as the physical body, lying with its feet sole to sole with yours. It lies out away from you. From your right temple imagine a line of energy that sweeps out horizontally in a semicircle

(Contd)

to join with the temple of the energy being. The line passes through the head of the energy being and sweeps round in a semicircle back to your left temple. When this image is a complete circle, imagine the energy being becoming brighter and brighter until it pulsates with pure white light, pure consciousness. At this moment imagine a flash of light from the head of the energy being, round the circle in an anticlockwise direction that passes through your head, at the temples, and back to the energy being. This lights up your mind connecting it with pure consciousness for the day. This can be repeated with the circle going through the heart of the physical and the energy being if you are feeling hurt, lost or lonely. Thank the energy being for switching on your light and let it return within your body.

10 THINGS TO REMEMBER

1 *Second Degree is essential training for practitioners.*

2 *It covers mental, emotional and distant healing.*

3 *Sacred symbols and mantras affect deep consciousness.*

4 *We can manifest thoughts by planting seeds of ideas in a still mind.*

5 *The power of intention creates a powerful focus.*

6 *There are only three symbols for Reiki Second Degree in the Usui system.*

7 *It is very important to ask permission when performing distant healing.*

8 *We can use affirmation to repattern the inner-self.*

9 *A group of students can send Reiki at a distance without being in the same location.*

10 *There is no place where I end and you begin. We are as one.*

11

Reiki Master's degree

In this chapter you will learn:
- *about the commitment of a master to both self-knowledge and inspiration of others, and the importance of choosing the right training and teacher for you*
- *about personal mastery through continued personal development, touching on what is necessary in Teacher Training.*

To listen to the heart is a challenge unparalleled.

Maharaj

Master's Level 1 – Personal Mastery

This is a level purely for personal growth. It only enhances practice on others by the deep lateral view that evolves through regular practice. Reiki is a spiritual discipline which must be practised as such at this level. This means that dedication and commitment are necessary, not only to the regular practice of self-treatment, but also to the investigation of the ways of energy and the meaning of consciousness.

Insight
It is one thing to look at what you do and try to change it. It is another to look at what you don't do. What often hurts

other people the most is when we don't listen, we don't see, we don't offer our services willingly without being asked. What have you left undone that affects the people around you? What more could you do to make those you are supposed to love feel more of that love and support?

The Master level is triggered by initiation, during which the Master's symbol is implanted in the heart of the student. The seed of light grows and shines from within. Inner light burns away all unwanted emotions from the past and present, leaving a clear state. When the light shines from within we obtain enlightenment. As long as we see the light shining on us from without then we will live with a dark shadow. A technique of activation and empowerment is taught prior to the initiation to prepare the student, like tilling the soil and feeding it well before the chosen seed is planted. The heart must be truly ready for this and open to the deeply sacred nature of the process.

The preparation exercise that I give is based on sound vibration to balance the energy/Chakra system and set it in motion to receive the implanting of the symbol and the mantra. Deep meditation arises after the mantra. The sound vibration is then repeated but in reverse to enable the earthing of the soul within the body.

The preparation technique is like a flower opening. Divine Spirit is called and welcomed. The completion technique envelops the changes and forms a new blueprint to cradle it in safety. When we lift our hearts and call upon the Divine White Light to enter, it surely does. Its grace is full of kindness and sensitivity. As the seed of light begins to grow from within the heart, Divine Love becomes the reward. There is absolutely no worldly gain in Master's Level 1. It is purely a personal enlightenment. It is hard to describe the changes as they are subtle, but all perceptions become pronounced and attachment to worldliness diminishes.

The sound vibration and techniques cannot be revealed in this book as it is unwise to perform them without proper guidance of an adept. Many people practise advanced techniques from books without first studying the preparation or gaining understanding. This is why each Degree should have an assimilation time of several months at least. Do not be in a hurry to proceed and look to what you already have. Stand still in simplicity and all will be revealed.

The sounds are particular to each energy centre and recreate the original state of balance in the centre that it would have had at birth. The embryo is in effect sung to by the universe in harmony and overtones known as morphic resonance. The sound changes the energy into physical substance that describes the vibration exactly in solid form. Energy becomes matter through mirroring the sound placed upon it. The sound is determined by the species, its current and historical DNA.

By impressing upon our weakened form the perfect primordial sound, the body is allowed to vibrate back into its original state of Being. The subsequent experience is one of light, joy and centred expansion. The sensation of coming home.

Daily practice followed by meditation and completion technique is recommended preceding the self-treatment programme. Enlightenment is yours, but you have to work for it!

There are only a handful of Masters who teach preparation and completion. The current energy exchange for Master's Level 1 is honoured, and dedication and commitment to practise is made. At least one year's preparation with Second Degree is recommended, two years are best. The course lasts one day only; review and journal keeping is encouraged.

METHOD TO INVOKE ENERGY

In Japan this technique is known as Hatsurei Ho. 'Hatsu' is to invoke or generate, 'rei' is spirit or energy and 'ho' is method or way – the 'method to invoke energy'. This was traditionally only given to teaching Reiki Masters but it is now taught at other stages. This method to invoke energy is performed by the teaching Reiki Master prior to initiating, and prior to their personal daily self-treatment. It is not taught at Reiki Level 1 or Reiki Level 2 as keeping things simple is best in the early stages. It will, however, be taught at Masters Level 1, Masters Level 2 and during the Empowerment through Advanced Reiki Practice programme for self-treatment.

1 *Posture – begin by standing in a relaxed posture or seated upright with the eyes closed.*
2 *Preparation – allow the mind a few moments to quieten.*
3 *Hand posture – 'Gassho' in Japanese, 'mudra' in Indian – hands together as if in prayer position. This aligns the energy forces in the hands, creating calmness and a focus back within the body.*
4 *Bow – as a sign of respect – open the hands out as if to receive something then repeat in the mind three times 'I open the door and enter'.*
5 *Intention – focus mental awareness on the present.*
6 *Energy sweep – place the right-hand palm at the left shoulder about an inch above the surface. Sweep down the body diagonally to the right hip and beyond in a gentle but sharp flicking motion (as in a martial art 'block'). Repeat three times.*
7 *Repeat with the left hand just above the surface from the right shoulder to the left hip and beyond. Repeat three times.*
8 *Place the right hand at the left shoulder with the left arm straight out in front, sweep down just above the surface of the arm energetically and flick off beyond the hand (on a bare arm this will feel like a wind blowing on the arm). Repeat three times.*
9 *Place the left hand at the right shoulder sweeping down as above. Repeat three times.*
10 *Both arms are raised straight above the head pointing to the sky without strain. Notice any sensations in the hands.*
11 *Place the hands in the lap, palms facing upwards. Notice any sensations in the hands.*
12 *Conscious breath – notice, without strain, as the breath comes in and goes out. Notice the point at which the breath turns from out to in and from in to out and is neither in nor out but*

suspended for a moment. The quieter the mind, the slower the breath and the longer the gaps will be.

13 *As the breath comes inwards, imagine breathing light from outside yourself, down through the top of the head into the whole body. Breathe out naturally and breathe in the light again for a further two breaths.*

14 *Breathe in as 13 but imagine the light radiating out through the hands on the out breath. Repeat for three breaths.*

15 *At this point the Reiki precepts can be repeated three times each on the out breath to remind yourself of your qualities (see Chapter 3).*

16 *Alternatively, just sit quietly and become aware of the energy within and in the hands.*

17 *Practise the self-treatment programme or the attunements at this point.*

18 *Hand posture – 'Gassho' as above. Repeat three times in the mind, 'I give thanks and close the door'.*

19 *Bow in completion and open the eyes.*

The downward flick in this method creates a flow of Chi down from the top of the arm and out through the hands in order to activate the Reiki for the treatment or attunements. In the finishing-off technique (see Chapter 8), the flick is generated upwards towards the heart in order to gather the energy back within the body and centre the person after the treatment.

Master's Level 2 – Teacher Training

The pathway to becoming a Reiki-teaching Master should be one of a long apprenticeship having first prepared with the appropriate intervals between First, Second and Third Degree. I would not begin to consider anyone for training until they had been practising Reiki for at least three years. The apprentice teacher will organize and assist on a minimum of six First Degree classes and four Second Degree classes and will attend all reviews. A teacher must also have clinical experience as they will be teaching many therapists, nurses, doctors, etc., and needs to have witnessed first-hand the effects of long-term treatment. In-depth case histories may be required. Practice on others gives insight into the many possibilities of how different people heal from the same symptoms or diagnosed illness in such different ways. Each person is wholly unique and symptoms cannot describe their personality or way of living accurately. For teaching, many principles must be realized that cannot simply be described.

It is important that the Master endeavours to remain fit, well and in balance to be an example to the student. They must be able to maintain their own strength and grounding through trust and faith in the practice of this system. They must present themself in a professional way. They need confidence and conviction which only comes about through the experience of a guided apprenticeship.

The undertaking of this all-consuming task must be gained over time by gathering a variety of opportunities to learn. Daily self-treatment is essential on all levels, not only for growth and understanding but also for protection as many energy vampires will unknowingly draw upon your giving field. It is essential to learn how to step back, leave alone, and when to move in and guide. Counselling skills are useful as emotions rise to the surface and may need to be discussed. This happens frequently and intensely during First Degree classes.

Practice management is necessary, as is knowledge of treatment/ training environment, equipment (you need several benches), ethics (non-discriminatory behaviour), group management, running of business, marketing, accounts, book-keeping, publicity and giving talks. Organization skills are also necessary to arrange classes and this is a prerequisite for apprentice Masters. It is not quite as easy as people just turning up. Students, before learning, need nurturing as great change is afoot and many have fears and apprehensions.

Principles must be learnt, understood, practised and maintained in the Master's own life. Standards must be kept and honour given.

The politics of Reiki in the world needs to be looked into and our attitude to it placed in balance. It may be enough to put you off completely! I shall not enter into politics here.

Our motivation must be clear and honest. We need to observe and assist on many classes of all the levels to know the form thoroughly: the technique, the principles and especially how to care for the needs of all possibilities for the student, such as the healing crisis (see page 148), anti-discrimination, respect of others' beliefs, group dynamics and many other responsibilities.

The teaching energy is embraced by the openness of the student's energy. The student is like a sponge for knowledge that can be transmitted only through their willingness to be open to this unique learning process. To facilitate learning the teacher must be aware of the openness and vulnerability of the student and treat them with the most humble respect. Advantage must not be taken of the student's trust. Learning how to engage a group energy and disengage again back to individual energy is something that comes only through practice.

The best start would be to gain a Teacher Training Certificate from your local college. The Reiki Master's programme is mostly about Reiki, whereas the college courses offer an understanding through practical experience and observation to teach confidently any number of people in any situation.

Legal aspects must be understood, insurance obtained for public liability and malpractice. Presentational skills need to be learnt and practised for introductory talks, interviews, demonstrations, etc.

Aftercare of the student must be on hand. Sharing groups can be set up where students can review the technique and discuss any questions or experiences. Second Degree students are usually skilled enough to do this, seeing the group organization as an honour.

The Master's exchange must be made over a mutually agreed time, say three years. The exchange was set by Takata in the late

1970s at $10,000 or the equivalent currency exchange in your area. This is a lot. The commitment is even greater than this as it is a lifetime. This amount is payable in instalments as the apprentice Master runs their own classes. So the Reiki generates the exchange for you. After completion of this task the apprentice is free of commitment to their trainer but never free of the commitment to uphold the principles of preparation, exchange, number of symbols, number of initiations, simplicity and the meaning of sacred.

Master's requirements – checklist

- *Reiki 1 Certificate with bona fide Master.*
- *Reiki 2 Certificate with bona fide Master not less that three months from Reiki 1.*
- *Fulfil practitioner requirements as set out in Chapter 12, pages 187–195.*
- *Complete apprenticeship training including Master's Level 1.*
- *Complete or commit to full Master energy exchange.*
- *Hold a teaching certificate.*
- *Have full malpractice and public liability insurance.*
- *Commit to continued professional development.*
- *Honour the commitment to confidentiality and ethics (Chapter 12, pages 189–191).*
- *Above all maintain a professional standard.*

Insight

Life's too serious not to be taken lightly. Care a bit less about what people think of you or you will trick yourself into being so serious that you miss the point and sacrifice joy.

Finding a suitable Master

If you want to take your knowledge of Reiki further and receive the initiations, you just have to 'ask and it shall be given unto you'.

Reiki will now appear from out of the woodwork and knock loudly on your door. If Reiki is not directly presented to you in your community by synchronicity then there are some useful addresses in the further information section at the back of this book. Membership of a Reiki association, organization or alliance does not necessarily guarantee quality of training or a correct understanding of energy by the Master. In Britain I can recommend the UK Reiki Federation with whom I am registered as a member. The Federation accepts all lineages of Reiki Master, practitioner or student who can prove their training and currently attempt to keep training and practice standards high. Some governing bodies require Anatomy and Physiology, First Aid Certificate, Teacher Training Certificate, practice management and counselling skills. The Reiki preparation and training lineage are also key factors. The Reiki Alliance in America is a worldwide organization set up by Takata and contains a large list of Masters. Beware of increasing politics, dogma and restrictions in all organizations. The Stillpoint School of Reiki upholds the principles of the original form of Usui Shiki Ryoho. Let intuition be your guide.

You will be drawn to the teacher you personally need by natural means if you are prepared to hold out for the best. If you wait, it will come to you but there are some useful guidelines for when you come across a number of different adverts in one magazine or on a noticeboard. Reiki has been diluted and amalgamated into many different forms. As far as I know, the Alliance still practise Usui Shiki Ryoho – the original form. If you do not yet have strong intuition or do not trust it then I list here some questions to ask of a Master's training, understanding and principles.

QUESTIONS TO ASK

▶ *What is Reiki? Can they be clear and concise?*
▶ *What is your historical lineage? They should be able to trace back in line to Dr Usui and not be more than five, six or seven in line from Takata.*
▶ *Do you teach the history of Reiki?*

- *How long was your training?*
- *How long was your apprenticeship?*
- *How much did you pay? If their energy exchange was only a few hundred pounds or dollars and their training a day or a weekend only, then they do not understand the quality of this energy.*
- *What is the name of your Master's Master?*
- *How soon after First Degree will I be able to take Second Degree and how much do these levels cost?*
- *Will I be able to take the Master's Level?*
- *Can I go into practice straight away?*
- *How many symbols do you teach for Second Degree and Master's Level 1? If more than three for Second or one for Master's then question the origin of these others and be doubtful about claims of channelling from Usui and Takata.*
- *How many initiations do you perform for each level? There should be four for First and one each for Second Degree and the Masters.*
- *Do you include the legs and feet in the finishing-off technique for grounding? This is asked as many teachers omit the legs and feet, thus leaving the receiver ungrounded and spaced out.*
- *How many Masters have you trained? One to three should have taken them through nine years of their practice. Be suspicious if this Master boasts 20 or, as one person writes proudly in a book full of symbols, several hundred.*
- *Have you been in public practice?*
- *Do you practise on yourself?*
- *Do you teach the five precepts?*
- *How much do you charge? Charges will vary from country to country but should at least be in line with any other professional training. The Master's apprenticeship is paid by organising classes for the current Master and commitment is made to paying the agreed fee. Hawayo Takata set the original fee at $10,000 in the late 1970s. It is generally open to negotiation.*
- *Do you take other forms of exchange?*

- *Do you belong to any Reiki organization?*
- *Are you insured to practise and teach? With whom?*
- *How many people are taught in a class? There should be no more than 12 for an individual teacher or 20 with a Second Degree assistant. Personal contact is imperative and cannot be given in groups of 50. Also, anyone entering a healing crisis on the course may need individual attention. I always have an assistant; it is also good experience for them.*

Ask for a trial treatment from the Master or one of their professional students. Experiencing Reiki first-hand is the best way to decide. Be prepared to travel: come to me, I will teach you.

Once booked on a class make your commitment to it, or rather to yourself, and stick to it. Don't let your car break down on the way, the cat get run over or spend the money on a new stereo instead in order not to make the change. It may be scary but remember, only fear dies.

> *That which is perfect has no reason to change for it is not seeking anything, it is in itself complete and perfect.*
>
> Maharaji

Questions and answers

Q *You have said what Reiki can do; are there any times when not to do it?*

A Don't do it on others when you are unwell or have an infectious or contagious disease. Don't treat anyone with mental illness unless you are used to this or qualified to do so. Don't undertake to treat someone terminally ill if you cannot face seeing it through. Treatment of organ transplants and pacemakers must be done with great caution or not at all. Don't treat anyone who is under the influence of drink or recreational drugs unless it is part of their recovery programme.

Q *I live alone and am on Income Support so I can't afford treatments. I did learn Reiki some years ago but lack confidence in giving it to people. What do you recommend for me?*

A It would be good for you to go to a sharing group of Reiki students in your area. If there isn't one then you can always call the people from your class and invite them to your place. This way you not only get to practice on others but receive treatment and have others with whom to discuss experiences. Don't be shy about this as they will be only too glad that someone else is doing the organizing. It may become a regular group. You may even like to host a class.

10 THINGS TO REMEMBER

1   *Personal mastery is a private discipline.*

2   *Physical postures and sound vibration prepare the physiology for the technique.*

3   *Meditation on the inner light brings about gradual awakening.*

4   *Hatsurei Ho activates and directs the Reiki for attunements and personal practice.*

5   *Teacher training is a lifetime's commitment.*

6   *The Master apprentice must honour the teaching and be devoted to daily practice.*

7   *The Master must live by the code of the five precepts.*

8   *The Master must be a working practitioner.*

9   *Choose your Master with care. Be sure they understand simplicity, silence and how to keep out of the way.*

10 *The Stillpoint School of Reiki offers regular treatments and training in a rural retreat in the Gloucestershire hills.*

12

Reiki in practice

In this chapter you will learn:
- *about the procedure involved in becoming a professional therapist, including ethics and guidelines*
- *how Reiki can be effectively integrated into other forms of therapy and health care.*

Leave no room for doubt in your mind.

Reiki as a therapy

Insight

The key to everything is breath. Breath is the difference between life and death. Breath does itself while you are busy doing something else. When the breath is free, you are free.

As much as self-treatment and treating others is important, receiving treatment from a professional Reiki therapist is extremely rewarding. Through professional training, the therapist will have gained other skills to help guide you through the process of healing and be able to explain the sensations and feelings that can arise. It is also of great comfort to share this experience within a safe environment where you can return, to go further, or deeper as you wish. Self-treatment is then invaluable to assist the process between treatments. The practitioner may be able to guide you to finding more courage and hope as the physical symptoms begin to lessen.

When undertaking treatment it is important to be open-minded as to the number of treatments needed and the length of time a healing may take. It may be leaps and bounds or it may be troughs and plateaux. Progress is made once trust of Reiki is gained through witnessing the energy moving in its special way.

It is important to note that after Reiki First Degree it is possible to practise a full body treatment on another person. This does not, however, give licence to beginners to take it upon themselves to become a Reiki therapist overnight. Even Takata proposed a long period of practical experience before embarking on treatment of people other than friends and family. She called the Second Degree 'the practitioner level', but this also should not be seen as the licence to practise straight away. Self-treatment and treatment of friends and family at Second Degree level should be undertaken for at least a year before beginning to think of Reiki as a therapy. There are many more things to consider than just the positions of a treatment.

Procedure

Before you think about setting up as a Reiki therapist, you should consider the following:

- *Perform daily self-treatment.*
- *Keep a journal of experiences and changes.*
- *Perform regular full treatments on others.*
- *Take people through a course of treatments, perhaps ten people through three to ten treatments each.*
- *Learn to take case histories and keeping notes of treatments on others.*
- *Commit to Second Degree with daily practice of distant healing.*
- *Undertake a programme of supervised treatments.*
- *Record case studies in a portfolio.*

- ▶ *Attend support groups and revision sessions as part of continued professional development.*
- ▶ *Complete and maintain a First Aid Certificate.*
- ▶ *Learn basic anatomy and physiology.*
- ▶ *Learn basic communication and counselling skills and study the client–therapist relationship.*
- ▶ *Set boundaries of time, commitment, exchange, professional relationship.*
- ▶ *Look into practice management – taking a course, investing in equipment, i.e. bench, covers, clinical rent, clothing, blanket, diary etc., accounts, book-keeping, record of money.*
- ▶ *Personal hygiene – no cigarettes or garlic, no strong perfume or incense.*
- ▶ *Business cards, leaflets, appointment cards.*
- ▶ *Become apprentice to a practitioner mentor.*
- ▶ *Insurance – check the laws in your country.*
- ▶ *Ethics – this is a very involved subject and must be looked into in detail.*

Ethics

Some basic ethical principles are:

- ▶ *Treatments are performed fully clothed at all times, apart from shoes.*
- ▶ *Confidentiality of client information is imperative to protect their rights and create a bond of trust.*
- ▶ *No personal credit is taken for the healing: remember self-empowerment.*
- ▶ *Do not diagnose or prescribe unless you are fully qualified to do so.*
- ▶ *Do not undermine the doctor's diagnosis or treatment.*
- ▶ *Never advise a client to stop medical treatment.*
- ▶ *Be aware of sexual barriers and never cross them: do not enter into sexual relations with clients, do not use any intimate*

positions, do not take advantage of the client's openness and vulnerability.

▶ Never claim to cure.

▶ Do not impose religious or political views on clients, yet respect theirs.

▶ Do not treat if you are unwell or have an infectious or contagious disease.

▶ When dealing with mental illness such as schizophrenia/psychosis, drink and drug addiction, always have a third party present. Never treat anyone who is knowingly under the influence of alcohol or recreational drugs unless this is part of an understood rehabilitation process. Have a third party present.

▶ Those who have taken recreational drugs in the past or practise a lot of meditation, yoga or Tai Chi may dip very deeply inwards, so grounding is imperative and possibly a shorter treatment.

▶ Refer the client to another therapist or therapy if you are unsure.

▶ Do not include movement of the hands; keep them still and non-invasive.

▶ Never refer to spirit guides, channel information, or negate the experiences of clients who do. There is a fine line between a spirit guide and possession by multiple spirits in mental illness. Do not entertain them in the session.

▶ Remain conscious, grounded and present, do not enter a trance state, or fall asleep, or allow your own issues to rise.

▶ Always use the finishing-off technique at the end of a session and give thanks to separate energy fields.

▶ Only use other therapies you are qualified and insured to practise, and inform the client of their use.

▶ Keep charges fair and reasonable but include an exchange of some sort. Free healing does not empower.

▶ Display certificates.

▶ Treat children only in the presence of their responsible parent/guardian and obtain written permission to do so. Check laws in your country and the Child Protection Act.

▶ Do not alarm the client with a negative or worrying manner, or comment during or after treatment. A deep relaxing state *may be produced where the client is open on a very deep level. Any words or action will be patterned very deeply. If you pick up a dense block do not assume you know what it is, you may be wrong. Simply refer the client to their doctor for a check. Do not let the ego rise in clairvoyance.*

▶ *Permission must always be obtained for healing. For those unable to give their own permission it is required from their responsible guardian. With animals it must be obtained from the owner, but check on the laws in your country as to whether you can treat animals at all.*

▶ *When working in hospital do not wear a white coat, and ask permission from the doctor in charge of the patient and the staff nurse in charge of the ward. Use curtains for privacy.*

▶ *Check if there are any regulations regarding the treatments of AIDs, HIV, Hep B, and sexually transmitted diseases which, in some cases, must not be undertaken for reward. Reiki does, however, benefit all these conditions and gives reassurance to the client of caring, through touch, which may have become a barrier for them. To those who no longer receive touch in their personal lives or who are afraid to touch others, Reiki gives the gift of deep comfort.*

▶ *Undertake to continue your personal spiritual growth through silence, meditation, reading, contemplation, ritual, journal and change of life habits.*

▶ *Do not enter into Reiki politics.*

▶ *Honour the principle of exchange.*

As a therapist it is not our place to divulge our insight into the client's illness, but knowing what we may know we can guide them towards the realization for themselves. Once they hit upon the understanding through their own experience the energy can shift and transformation instantly occurs. The therapist must guide towards the gift, not give the answers.

Treatment in practice is more involved than just the simple laying on of hands with the intention to heal. So firstly practise on yourself, friends and family and gain confidence through the deep insight that will grow in you. Also it is wise to receive regular treatment from someone else. I do this myself by swapping with a friend and really notice the difference on the weeks she and I are too busy to get together.

Reiki as a complement to other therapies

> **Insight**
> Reiki supports and enhances all medical treatment, being used effectively by conventional doctors, complementary practitioners and by everyday people such as you or I.

Reiki is a complete system in itself. Additional techniques are not usually necessary as all utilize the same Universal Life Force. All complementary therapies aim to rebalance the energy by using different methods and principles but see the person as a whole. They too look into the habits of the person, their likes and dislikes, their emotional history as well as the physical symptoms. All things together create the map of the individual in the state of current imbalance. Many people who learn Reiki go on to learn other forms of therapy and many people come to learn who already practise (I also have a diploma in Indian Head Massage and am a certified practitioner of Emotional Therapy). The main importance is to note that their common experience is that Reiki becomes a protection for them during their other treatments, which, with massage, chiropractic, etc., can be quite tiring. Each practitioner has the gift to regenerate their own energy before, during or after treatment on another.

Many therapists use the Reiki in combination with their other forms of therapy and thus personal therapies evolve. Each person is drawn to a different combination of systems that they are led to by their own personal journey. As Reiki never leaves, it is available in the hands at all times and may come through during aromatherapy, reflexology or Zero Balancing treatments. Some practitioners like to keep each therapy separate and evolve from one skill to another as the client is ready for it. Sometimes it is found that some structural manipulation or alignment is useful before Reiki in order to allow deep healing to occur. I personally find that structural blocks can slow down the process quite dramatically. Generally, with trust and patience, the Reiki will shift all the levels. Reiki assists the integration of other systems and the smooth transition from illness to health.

Reiki is recommended to clients by counsellors of many forms: psychosynthesis, transactional analysis, emotional therapy, psychodrama, brief therapy, neuro-linguistic programming (NLP), hypnotherapy, and so on. By practising self-treatment daily the emotions and issues that arise during therapy can be integrated without such pain. Reiki transforms energy from one form to another without the need for the individual issue or memory being accessed. Many deep-seated blocks can leave the system without the need for them to be unearthed in the present only to cause the opening of a huge can of worms. The past can be such a pit of pain for some people but the transition can be eased with Reiki as it leads the Being and the body towards the light.

Reiki can enhance our ability for channelling, clairvoyance, mediumship, telepathy, intuitive interpretation of Runes, Tarot and palmistry. Our basic insight awakens to see and know all things.

Reiki is used hand in hand with orthodox medicine by those brave enough to challenge the limitations of science. It has been found useful with therapies such as radiotherapy, chemotherapy, physiotherapy, hydrotherapy, vitamin therapy, nutritional therapy and general medical drug therapy. It helps patients reduce their stress levels, detoxify their systems and heal their injuries or illnesses more rapidly. The side-effects of chemotherapy and radiotherapy can be eased, including nausea, anxiety, exhaustion and the tension in scar tissue.

Recovery from surgery can be quite surprising, especially when the treatments begin some weeks before medical treatment commences. This prepares the person, the body and especially the site for the trauma. Treatment after surgery speeds up the tissue regeneration, easing shock and bruising. Distant Second Degree Reiki can be very effective in these circumstances. It gives the person waiting at home a valid role to play in an otherwise helpless situation.

Reiki experience varies from person to person, but it never ceases to amaze me how such a simple thing can produce such a profound effect that not only heals the physical wounds but changes people's lives into ones of joy and fulfilment. Treat yourself, take it further.

> *When my heart fills with gratitude it is one of the most wonderful feelings of life.*
>
> Maharaji

Questions and answers

Q *I have had one treatment but the pain got worse. Could you tell me why?*

A This happens from time to time. It is the pain's return from a deep place of suppression and the body's ability to adapt itself, in order not to feel the pain, that allow the pain to resurface during or after treatment. This should subside after a few days. Further treatment is recommended to shift the trauma.

Q *I would really like to give up smoking but when I try I get really jittery and put on weight. Can Reiki help?*

A Reiki treatment and self-treatment can certainly help but ultimately will-power has to be acquired also. Self-treatment gives you the ability to focus on your own well-being and create affirmations to change your habits. The weight can balance out also as you gain control of your emotions. Daily treatment is recommended but use the finishing-off technique whenever you feel out of control. It also occupies the mind and the hands.

Q *I am going to Africa next year and worry about vaccination. Can Reiki help?*

A This subject is open to debate. It has to be your choice to vaccinate or not and your responsibility to accept the consequences of that choice. If the body is strong and has a healthy immune system Reiki can keep the energy high so diseases are less likely to be attracted. Use common sense, or simply go somewhere else.

Q *Why do people Reiki their food? This looks a bit fanatical to me.*

A Some people like consciously to bless their food with Reiki to clear any energetic impurities. My personal view on this is to eat organic or fresh food wherever possible or grow your own. It is more about how we assimilate the food than what it is.

Q *I have arthritis. What can I expect from a treatment?*

A It is most probable that the pain will ease and the joints will feel freer. The warmth of hands during healing is very soothing. It may be that the diet needs to be looked at also.

Q *My uncle has had his leg amputated from the knee down and says he gets a lot of pain in the foot that isn't there. How do I treat him?*

A Do a full body treatment but imagine a leg and a foot when you get to that part. The physical leg has gone but the energetic leg still remains as an extension of the brain signals in the aura. Spend some time over the stump area to relax the scar tissue and trauma.

The future is made from choices at the crossroad of this moment, so consciously change and the future will be your fulfilment.

10 THINGS TO REMEMBER

1 *Reiki as a therapy should be kept separate from other techniques.*

2 *Silence allows the client a new experience away from the world.*

3 *The body will tell you how many treatments to have.*

4 *There is more to professional practice than just doing the treatment.*

5 *The ethical code protects both the client and the practitioner.*

6 *The code of conduct stresses the importance of confidentiality.*

7 *Counselling or Emotional Therapy training is helpful if people have issues they wish to discus as part of their healing.*

8 *Reiki speeds up the recovery from operations and illness.*

9 *Reiki changes lives.*

10 *Reiki can amplify the benefits of other forms of therapy.*

13

Experiences with Reiki: the students speak

In this chapter you will learn:
- *about the changes that can take place from either treatment or training and the intense gratitude students have for the gift*
- *about the students' experiences as inspiration as they express from the heart.*

He who really knows today, and the heart of today, knows its parent yesterday and its child tomorrow.

Charles Johnson

Insight

People do not have to learn Reiki in order to continue with life the way it has always been, yet if they are curious enough to try it for themselves, they may find life soon changes for the better.

WILL KAY

I have just celebrated ten years being clean as a heroin addict in recovery. I remember when you [Sandi] came to my mum's house to do a Reiki weekend. On the Friday evening I was upstairs while your group of Reiki trainees were practising their Second Degree downstairs. I woke up on the Saturday morning to you handing me a cup of tea in my room where I was surrounded by my needles and general trappings of my disease. That night you gave me a treatment and the next day I spent searching the internet for a rehab centre. A week later I entered the rehab and my awakening began.

Soon after that day you made a dedication to me in your book. You wrote: 'To William. May Reiki hold your soul until you see it clearly for yourself.' Later you gave me Reiki Second Degree as a gift for surviving recovery. I am glad to say that since then I have allowed a higher power/the universe/Reiki to guide me and am now able to look after myself. I am in my final year of Chiropractic college. I can't quantify in any scientific sense how much all the Reiki that was sent to me helped, but I can say that I felt carried through a hard time in my life. (Will is now a qualified Chiropractor with a thriving business. He is happily married and baby Max was born in March 2009.)

PAUL MCBRIDE

Mht DHP MBAThH MBBNLP, Integrated Therapist of Mind Body Spirit, three times world kickboxing champion.

I first came across Sandi and Reiki when my search for something else began, at least that is how I understood it then. In fact it was something else seeking me. I was going through an extremely traumatic time and had been for a very long time.

I had very real events going on in my life, the effects that these events had on me were catabolic. When people say stress can kill, I could really feel it; every cell of my body felt as though I was dying. I was asking God – the universe – a higher power, 'Why is this happening to me?' 'When will this go away?' 'Will it ever stop?'

I could only see two ways of it ever going away: by either me going against all my values and being someone I did not want to be; or to trust in God – the universe – a higher power. Every day I would have momentary feelings of giving up; it was so hard in so many ways, unexplainable in a few words. During this negative time,

I had developed or been given as a gift, a heightened awareness. This was needed for the events happening in my life and was totally appreciated, but I was permanently in this state of heightened awareness. This was not always nice. I could sense people's emotion and intention, and in the very few minutes of sleep I would get I could hear a pin drop a mile away. I could not switch off and wind down.

Then during all this, just as I would notice negative so-called coincidences, I started to notice strangely obvious positive coincidences. They were like signs or clues, each one leading to the next, really miraculous. It was like something or someone was trying to show me and guide me to places; my intuition was spot on and I began to feel like I was being looked after.

A series of these signs led me to Sandi's book, each sign so clearly leading to the next; miracles were really happening, I would be in places I had no idea I was going to be and I would bump into signs, etc. I ended up in a library when I was out with someone and they suddenly remembered they needed to pop into the library. I was waiting around by one of the bookshelves and I decided to look on the shelf, and Sandi's little blue book was placed there; it was not in its proper location and was among books of a totally different subject. Now, one would normally think or believe that this was just coincidence, but around a week previously I had been led miles away from home by these miraculous so-called coincidences, one of which was speaking to a lady who told me I was going to do some healing, probably Reiki.

I got the book out of the library and read it; I contacted Sandi and told her what I was going through and asked if I could come and learn Reiki. Sandi invited me to do so and the experience was amazing – it gave me a true sense of belonging and reuniting. I went home and, as instructed by Sandi, gave myself Reiki every day for months. This was amazing, I no longer could feel my self dying but I could actually feel myself healing and recharging. The events in my life were still there but I could cope a lot better. Sandi was also there for me, and would also send me Reiki.

Reiki was what had been missing from my life for quite some time. Now Reiki was in my life I could reach that final step where before I had fallen short. Since I was a young lad I have been doing martial arts and in recent years before Reiki came to me I had reached world championship level, but fell short of becoming world champion. I had all the skills and ability, I had the positive mental attitude, but there was something missing in me – Reiki.

The year I took Reiki 1, I went to the World Kickboxing Championships in Killarney in Ireland. I gave myself Reiki in my rest periods between training weeks before and immediately prior to competing. I just had this knowingness that I was going to win, and I did, I became world champion. I did the same the following year in Basel, Switzerland and the next year in Niagara Falls, Canada. Winning world championships in 2003, 2004, 2005, and as I write I am current World Champion.

I have been able to do this because Reiki has made me more complete. I now have an understanding of everything I have been through and agree with what a person once said to me: 'This is all happening to you to make you into what you are going to be.' I now fully understand this and I am now an Integrated Therapist of Mind Body Spirit, and following in similar footsteps to Sandi by helping others. Sandi has always been there for me and I appreciate that; I have learnt so much from her and our friendship and I hope to help people in a similar way, with an unconditional love towards all.

SUSANNE

I had been involved with therapies for many years and Reiki had been one of the mysteries that I felt I needed to experience. I began to feel real burning and aching in my inner palms and felt this was drawing me towards using my hands more directly – I am an acupuncturist and more used to using needles. Reiki is so gentle and uncomplicated, does not need explanation or a reason, but simply draws you closer to your own stillness and simplicity. It is wonderful as a way of holding, comforting and acknowledging another person's fragility; it is a gentle glow that can warm, nourish and rekindle. Personally, Reiki has helped me feel less alone.

MARY

I came to Reiki through having Chronic Fatigue Syndrome. Having meditated since I was 18, and feeling a need to deepen my spiritual life, it seemed the perfect thing to try. I took Reiki 1 a couple of years ago and as soon as possible I took Reiki 2.

I have self-treated daily since then and found great benefits on physical, emotional and spiritual levels. My health has improved hugely – Reiki is a continual support to my system and therefore my energy levels. It calms in moments of worry or crisis, increases confidence and clears and eases the mind. I find a greater connection with the world and somehow feel a connection with the universe through using its energy and being gratefully aware of what it can do for us. This connection is very apparent when treating other people and it is wonderful to see their reaction to receiving such a simple process even when they don't really know what Reiki is.

JENNY

My Reiki journey began six years ago by pure chance. I wandered into a major bookstore and was drawn to the complementary therapy section and idly picked up a book about Reiki. Not knowing at the time what it was I sat down and began to read; I couldn't put it down. I was completely immersed in what I was reading until an assistant came to me; she asked if I was going to buy the book as they were not a library. I bought the book and from that moment on my life changed. The author of the book was Sandi Leir-Shuffrey who became my Reiki Master.

Reiki has led me to treat Multiple Sclerosis (MS) sufferers and the disabled, which is a very humbling experience. They are so brave and expecting, and love the weekly sessions giving them empowerment for just a short while. I have grown so much from my experience with Reiki, it has made me understand the true essence of life and opened up my mind to the purity and clarity of the universe. Whenever I feel anxious, Reiki takes me gently by the hand to a tranquil place of safety where I can treat myself in peace and light.

JULIA

Reiki has given me the strength to move forward and put the past behind me. By learning to treat myself, Reiki is always there helping me and showing me the way. A great change took place from the very first treatment.

MRS O

My husband and I were involved in a car accident about nine months ago. It was tremendously stressful as we were both injured and felt quite emotionally neglected. We are in our seventies. I was drawn to the book and instantly knew this was for us. I had been left with acute anxiety, panic and distress as well as feeling wretched. We braved the two-hour journey and first received a treatment from Sandi, which was so deeply calming. The next day we joined two lovely people, also on a journey to healing, and received the Reiki 1 training. Everyone said how I had changed in just two days. Indeed, I felt so much better, my confidence had returned and I felt so happy and excited for the first time in ages. I had less pain in my arthritis and felt more flexible. The Reiki was so easy to do, even with my bent fingers. My husband feels he now has a tool with which he can help me and I can give some back to him. It's another way of showing our love, I suppose. I will always be grateful to Reiki for waking me up again. When we have practised for a while, we intend coming back for more.

CARMEL

Reiki 1 was the most beneficial and enjoyable weekend. I chose to train with Sandi as she is in direct lineage from Dr Usui. Since practising daily self-treatment, I have noticed remarkable changes to my health. The last year had been very traumatic for me and

I was under such a lot of stress. I was having panic attacks when I was out walking and I had a lot of very painful muscle spasms from an accident over 20 years ago. I never felt relaxed.

The panic attacks have now stopped; I have hardly any muscular pain and feel so much calmer than I have felt for a long time. The dry sore patches that I had on the back of my knees for years every winter have disappeared. For me, Reiki is a wonderful gift that I shall now use every day of my life. I am delighted to be doing Reiki 2 in a few days' time.

CAROLINE N

When I broke may ankle badly I resisted Reiki as everything was all too much. I had two metal plates fitted which created an infection in the wound. The antibiotics I was given made me really ill and depressed. As I am usually very active and self-employed, the accident gave me a great shock. After some weeks of deep pain and much frustration I had a little Reiki on my ankle through the plaster and was very surprised to feel heat tingling and strange sensations in my foot. The colour of my toes improved as the swelling was noticeably improved. The plaster was in fact removed quite early for such a break but the pain and discomfort did not seem to change. I was constantly taking painkillers.

After about ten weeks I was offered a full Reiki treatment as things weren't progressing well. Sandi worked mostly on my head, neck, upper back and released the shoulder joints. A short time was spent on the actual injury that was still very swollen, raging with heat, and purple. I was still using crutches as I couldn't put my toe on the floor. My whole body had become twisted to compensate for the pain. After the treatment the heat had gone, all but a tiny patch on the top of my foot; the colour had changed to a reasonable pink and the swelling was definitely improved.

Next day was my visit to the physiotherapist and she couldn't believe the difference. I found I had about 50 per cent flexibility again. My ankle bones were once more visible and the swelling had improved even more. My posture had straightened and I felt in balance again. Two days later I secretly got into my car and tried the clutch pedal which before had been impossible to use but I managed to hold it down firmly with no pain at all.

For the first time in three months I could pick my son up from school without relying on other people. I must honestly say I was amazed at what happened and am now back at work. I don't know what took me so long to receive the Reiki: maybe I was afraid it wouldn't work. I'm glad I did.

MARY R

I lead a very busy life as a professional horsewoman. I travel a lot and put my body through extremes with little time for recovery. For many years I have had pains in my face and breathing difficulties. I have had a lot of dentistry over the last 12 months but this seems to have made the situation worse. I was offered a treatment by a lady I met at the polo club. After the first treatment which, I must say, was wonderfully relaxing, she told me that I must go to the doctor and have my sinuses checked out as she had picked up some energy changes there. I wasn't sure what she meant but went to the doctor. I was referred to the specialist and after an X-ray it was found that I had a huge benign tumour in my left sinus area. I was operated on the next day and have since recovered fully. I can now breathe easily and the face pain has gone. I have also noticed that the movement in my legs has improved. It is a great skill when the practitioner can detect such changes in the energy that she knows when something is wrong. I am fascinated by it all and hope to learn for myself so I can do self-treatment and also treat my horses.

MRS A

I had a regular life until 1993 when I had an episode of extreme stress and anxiety brought on by the stresses and demands of my job. My father died after an illness, I had to support my mother through this rough time, my children were taking exams and to top it all I lost my job. I gradually resumed work at a new post, my mother became more dependent on me, my children left home, my relationship with my husband then deteriorated to such an extent that we seriously considered divorce in March 1999.

Reiki 1 had become important in my daily life. Having learnt it in 1996 I use it on myself, and to enhance my reflexology and aromatherapy clients' treatments. Reiki works particularly well for me at night and in the morning: I often fall asleep halfway through my self-treatment routine.

I learnt Reiki 2 in April 1999 and used it on myself daily. On reflection it seemed to speed up the difficult situation. My husband began to show serious signs of stress, making a decision to save our sanity vital. I asked, through the Reiki, to be given guidance to help our situation and love.

One day my Reiki Master phoned and out poured all my concerns and worries not previously expressed to her or anyone. Once the initial step had been taken to talk, I found I was able to talk to other close family members. It was a release to talk and have their support and love.

Reiki opened up channels of personal communication within me, and there is much now to do. I use and trust the Reiki and am constantly amazed at the openings and coincidences and events that simply occur, bringing change, enhancement and love to our lives.

JOHN B

For me, I think Reiki has helped me discover peace and tranquillity within and it has been great for self-development and learning. It helped a dog of mine which had an injured shoulder. It definitely brought relief and he loves a hand on his shoulder now.

PETE S

Reiki has been the other piece in the jigsaw. It's like God has given a gift to the world and had brought it to the fore now for an increase in energy for the healing of people. Since doing Reiki 1 I have been more aware of the movement of energy and a quickening of energy in the spiritual sense, and it has left me with the feeling of urgency in the spirit, as though something new is happening and I am being told to hurry to connect to it. It has led me in a new direction where I am free to help.

On a healing level it has been invaluable in helping my mother as she was really poorly, and I know she would be unable to continue to live on her own without it. It is something I can give back to her. That feels good. I have also noticed that people with ailments talk to me about their illnesses as though I can do something for them. Even though they don't know I do Reiki, it's like some force is bringing them for healing, but my main growth has been spiritually.

MRS C

Reiki helps me to stay calmer. It gave me something positive to do when I was regularly waking at night. It proved more effective at getting me back to sleep than a number of other strategies I had tried.

I use it on my two dogs who are both old and ill. It seems to calm them. One of them will only accept it when he is really agitated – it seems to calm him and then he rests. The other is keen to receive at any time – he's always hated being held by anyone.

Insight

Eventually, the lack of fulfillment leads people to search for ways to regain happiness. They reach out and find that the answer is in their own hands. It was there all along.

J A

I am better able to cope with life's ups and downs. I am always surprised at the direction I end up taking and it is often completely the opposite to that which I would have chosen. However, with the benefit of hindsight, it is the best path. I am a much happier person since doing Reiki.

My cat used to walk away from me if I so much as looked at her and yet after the first session of Reiki she came to me and now insists on sitting on my lap at every opportunity. This says to me that something has changed; it must be in me, it must be in the energy that I feel and that I now give out.

CHRIS H

I asked a friend for Reiki after my son died. It was a beautiful experience and next day I woke up knowing that I would be able to carry on – it was very powerful knowledge, which enabled me to go onwards. Reiki did this for me.

RUBY

I started to learn Reiki to help my son who has MS, but discovered it helped me and somehow changed my life, although it is hard to describe in what way. My perceptions of myself somehow seem to have changed.

My daughter also did Reiki training with me and we seem to have a closer bond. She responds very well to my hands on. What a gift.

SARAH B

It seems a long time since I learnt Second Degree Reiki. I have used it successfully on myself, animals, children, friends, a tree, and by distance on situations with my family, friends, and a few people with bad health. I have not gone around promoting it in an evangelical manner, but it is amazing how suspicious and frightened some people are!

As for sensation – on myself, First Degree seemed to work most strongly on my throat and heart, Second Degree on the head.

My hands usually feel a sort of 'electric' tingling and so does the part receiving the treatment. When I was trying to treat my dying cat I felt a dead coldness, I thought someone had left a door open. Sometimes I feel a shivering sensation in my upper back.

When I am treating other people I seem to pick up a 'whizzy' feeling if I get the right spot. I also frequently get a strong feeling of the emotional state of the person, and a corresponding feeling of compassion in myself. This occurs even if I don't like the person much!

My feelings about Reiki have changed as time has passed: to start with I considered it as some kind of unexplained phenomenon and rather ignored the initiation side of it. It certainly seemed to work, and I have to go on experience and direct knowledge as I distrust elaborate belief systems. Since the Second Degree initiation I feel that it is much more of a spiritual thing and this recognition has led me strangely but firmly through doubts and depression (and some strange coincidences) to the knowledge that I still have to struggle continually with my own journey and not to expect Reiki to muffle all the pain. At times, my feelings of knowing people intuitively and of experiencing so many extremes of feelings from everywhere in the world press upon me to the point of being unbearable, despite activities such as writing poetry or meditating or gardening, etc.

I have days when I feel people are somewhat suspicious of me, and others where people unaccountably gravitate towards me as though in search of something (healing?). I know some people think I am crackers, but I could be just clumsily grappling with the path of life as I suppose one is meant to.

My confidence has grown, particularly in the respect that I am now able to show that I am interested in a caring way in other people, and I find people tell me things about their health or ideas about life. I don't really know if Reiki has affected what 'psychic abilities' I have; perhaps it is more a case of opening a clear way for existing deep knowledge to flow. My intuitive 'powers' do seem to be strengthening, though.

Things keep changing all the time, and I am much happier now.

SUE, JOHN, KEIRA R

1994. Thank you for a wonderful weekend at which we gained so much. In fact, Keira said she gained more in two days than in all her school life! We have already started to use our gift of Reiki today by giving John's mum a full treatment and John gave her dog a treatment also, which they both loved. So this is the beginning of something wonderful.

As a family, my husband and daughter, who was nearly 16, and I joined in at a caring sharing weekend in August 1994, where we were free to sample different complementary therapies in give and share sessions. Our daughter received a short head and shoulders session of Reiki and came away wanting to know more. So as a sixteenth birthday present for her we all went along to Sandi for a weekend attunement in the First Degree of Reiki, followed some months later by Second Degree.

I have been asked to give Reiki to several people who have been very unwell and it has most definitely 'kick started' their recovery or given them a sense of inner peace they had been lacking, or reduced significantly the pain they have been in, which then lets them help themselves. In every giving and receiving situation the Reiki energy seems to come through to help.

Our daughter uses the Reiki to help her friends and through the Reiki has picked up on operations they have had in the past, which she knew nothing about, and another friend with psoriasis which was helped.

We also use Reiki within the family, and to bring assistance in situations, the most recent of which was a university work place module which was proving difficult to organize, until we started using Second Degree on the situation. The very next telephone call went perfectly smoothly, with us being able to talk to the person concerned, who now had the time, and wanted to speak to my daughter, and everything was arranged in minutes.

I use Reiki in combination with my reflexology during which the energy just comes and flows in these situations. It is wonderful. The clients frequently comment on the lovely tingly feelings up their legs from the feet at the tuning in the Reiki.

SALLY

Thank you for sending me Reiki. You have helped me find some inner strength. I have never managed to feel life force before, even after having three or four Reiki treatments with other people. What did you do?

ANNE L

Learning Reiki seems like the best thing I have ever done.

LARA

I just wanted to thank you for helping me change my life! It's Ace! I now feel brilliant because I'm at last doing what I've always wanted to do. I've got a wonderful feeling of wholeness that I've never had before; I always felt empty and now I'm filling up!

ANNA

A lot has happened since the Reiki weekend which culminated in my having the courage at last to leave home. I had been unhappy for so long but had never told a soul. I moved well away from the farm as it had been such a burden for me. The children are all settled with their respective partners and children and appreciate the help I can give to their aches and pains, especially the grandchildren when they stay. They always return home healthier and calmer. Reiki/Granny's love – same thing!

CAROL P

When I learnt Reiki my intention was to help other people but little did I know what I was going to have to go through first.

Since my accident I have used Reiki on myself so much and it has been extremely beneficial for me. It has brought me so much peace and calm. It has also made me more relaxed than I ever thought possible, and I am more positive and not so worried about the future, even though on a bad day I don't like what I see very much.

GILLIAN OSMANT

I had heard of Reiki three or four times before but had put it aside, although it sounded lovely. Then one day a leaflet appeared in reception and the rest is history!

I remember the feeling of a peaceful coming home as I learnt the hand positions and received Reiki for the first time. At the initiation I felt sick and shaky but then came this wonderful white light and although I am a Christian there was a Buddha in gold surrounded by white light and a feeling of immense peace. I felt I wanted to hug the world afterwards.

I practised on myself and family and was amazed at the results that occurred. My husband found immense relief from tiredness; my son, who was rather sceptical, relaxed visibly as I gave him a full treatment and he even fell asleep. My youngest daughter also fell asleep within five minutes of being on the table and woke up without her headache.

I later took Second Degree during which the light came again and was much more intense and clear. I have changed since my Second Degree and can cope with life much better and feel intense love for people now.

JOY

I had been in a deep depression for over 12 months, under the care of a psychiatrist. Medication had had severe side-effects. At this point in time, I was introduced to Reiki by a friend. Although sceptical as conventional treatment wasn't working for me, I had nothing to lose by trying alternative therapy.

I went along to my first appointment full of trepidation, not knowing what to expect. Immediately I was put at my ease, meeting a warm and friendly person. I was unaware at this time that she was to play a large part in my recovery from depression.

After my first session I had complete faith that Reiki was going to help me. I felt more relaxed and at ease with myself, not realizing then that I was about to begin a voyage of self-discovery.

Facing up to my past hasn't been an easy path to travel as it has been very rugged in parts. Working in partnership with my Reiki therapist, I've found the courage the carry on. By attending regularly for Reiki therapy, little by little I am able to see more clearly.

It is helping me to unravel the past and let it go, to look at my past problems logically and not through emotions. Yes, at times I have cried in the process of letting go, but it is all part and parcel of the healing process. Slowly and surely I've begun to take down the wall that has surrounded me for over ten years, letting go of the guilt that I'd allowed others to build upon.

SALLY

The first thing I noticed after Reiki was that everything was *really, really green*! I mean *really green*! All the colours outside had become more clear and vivid. That first night I was cooking dinner and was amazed at how green the broccoli was! It sounds a strange thing to notice but my perception had become so heightened.

Sometimes I am not sure I have got it right but I know Reiki has been a great support to me. Before learning I could never sit by myself, I would have to go out, go for a run, call someone, but now I can lie down and be still with myself as I do Reiki: this is a miracle to me. I can honestly say that Reiki has been the best investment I have ever made.

I felt I wanted to take the training further but was out of work and struggling with my life, then sadly my grandmother died and left me the exact amount needed to take Second Degree. It was just what I was looking for, I felt that my dear grandmother had given me life again.

I have used Second Degree all the time for myself and my situations. It gives me confidence and courage to face my fears. My boyfriend was looking for a new house for ages to no avail, so I sent some Reiki to this situation for him. That evening he phoned me to say he had seen a house and within five minutes of being there had bought it! I feel a lot of feedback from Second Degree; it gives a different dimension and shows me not to rush in to help people, but to be patient and help without interfering.

MICHAEL W

I am working with a neighbour, a lady of about 60, who is pretty fit but has recurring back problems. I work with her on the treatment couch, going over the usual hand positions, but concentrating for an extra few minutes on the particular area where the pain is and ending with the finishing-off process, which seems to be very important. She always feels very much better afterwards and sleeps very well. She reports that it feels as though she had a hot water bottle strapped to her back for several days afterwards!

I realized the importance of the finishing-off technique when I once omitted it. The lady felt very drowsy, distant and reported palpitations. I realized that she had become ungrounded so next time I completed the form after which she felt marvellous.

DR DAVID B

The younger David was very different from the 'post-Reiki' David. He was proud to be a junior doctor. He was an obsessive perfectionist, painfully shy and socially isolated. He worked the usual 100–120 hour week, getting no sleep for days on end yet obsessively weight training, forcing down gallons of body builder powder, and getting even less sleep chasing around the country after a hopeless relationship. He tried to be the strength of the family when his sister was partially paralysed with meningitis. He was also studying to further his career. His mood swings, bouts of inconsolable crying and suicidal thoughts were the norm, he thought, until he found himself having increasing fear and panic, paralysing fatigue, muscle aches and other signs of 'burn out'. He once crouched on the end of his bed overwhelmed with fatigue and fear, wondering if he might be going mad.

On and off, David spent six months in bed and was left with chronic fatigue. His psychiatrist put his depression down to chemical changes and prescribed a long course of antidepressants. He was told that he would always have problems with anxiety. His counsellor suggested a career change. He felt that drugs would cover up the cause of the problem and still blamed others for his condition: the bosses, the system, the psychiatrist, the GP, the ex-relationship, the family.

He felt insulted by the way his profession was treating him and began to put his energy into exploring other ways of healing. He explored NLP, journey work, Transcendental Meditation, a job of only 38 hours per week, but still he felt stuck with the fatigue and loss of passion for life. He tried homoeopathy, reflexology and diets, all of which helped but never reached the core.

He came across Reiki but at first thought it too weird. The symbol intrigued him and he was led to take Reiki 1. He describes the course as 'freeing, enlightening, hilarious, scary, fun and very, very right'. He began to laugh uncontrollably from the beginning as he felt his heart open. Self-treatment began and continued daily. He felt changes and sensations in his hands and body. His energy levels began to rise, his clarity and calm returned. He began to offer his gift to his wife and family who responded well. He was amazed at how just a few minutes' Reiki could take away pain and bring relief. He continued to have monthly treatments with his Reiki Master.

Sixteen months on he is unrecognizable even to himself. He says, 'My heart feels open and free, I am blessed with a beautiful wife who has stayed by me and believed in me. I have a new career in which I am passionately growing month by month. I have enrolled on a diploma course and am part way through an MSc in psychotherapy. I am also working as a doctor yet keen to challenge the world of medicine on its shortcomings. I am once again able to enjoy regular jogging and walks.

'I am joyful at the periods of peace and happiness that I now feel, the connection with others and the ability to feel passion and love again. Confidence is a new and welcome friend. My wife and I are training for a trek next year to Everest base camp!'

Instead of feeling lost and detached, David now feels whole, present and happily on the right path. 'Reiki has been the catalyst for the quantum change that happened in my life. Experiencing and practising Reiki produced a huge shift in my belief systems about what is possible. I feel in a position of balance, understanding and free energy.' David is sad that ethics and politics at work do not allow for him to use Reiki there, yet.

SARA N

I suffer from anxiety and panic attacks with bouts of deep depression that come as if from out of the blue, like a descending cloud. I have learnt Reiki for self-treatment and use it daily. When I feel one of my bad weeks creeping up I step up the treatment. It is such a comfort in such a scary place to have my own hands as the tool for healing. The heat generated is tremendous and gives me a sense of warmth and peace. I can hold the panic with my hands until the anxiety begins to lessen. On the outside I appear strong and confident but inside I struggle. Now I have a trusty friend.

BRENDA

The first time I heard about Reiki I had been ill for about two years. I had visited my doctor and had lots of tests: the result was that 'everything was all right'. I became very distressed, I made up my mind that I had no more interest in my life. Yes, I had given up. Then came the turning point.

I was put in touch with a lady who practised reflexology. When I told her how ill I felt her calm voice put me at ease and she asked me if I had heard of Reiki. The word sounded magical. She said it was a healing method by laying hands on you and taking in energy. I became more interested. I have been seeing this lady for more than two years now. In my mind I call her 'Misty' – I need to get to the other side of the mist to find out more about Reiki.

Once you have learnt the art of relaxing you will never look back. You will be like me, in control of your body.

Yes, that is how I see Reiki, I call it educating my mind. At this stage I am hooked. You must always have faith and never give up. I know, I have been there, and with help from 'Misty' yes, I have won.

I still have bad days, but with the magic word Reiki and my faith I cope quite well. It has given me my confidence back and taught me not to worry about things I can do nothing about. I often go to a quiet part of the house, lie down and relax, and pull in as much energy as I can for about half an hour. I feel much better and refreshed. This is why you should go to good Reiki classes and learn the art of Reiki from the beginning. It will be your secret.

I have been diagnosed as having Parkinson's Disease while I have been studying Reiki, so you see without it I would not be the strong person I am today. I have completed the First Degree. Reiki is a wonderful way to good health and a clear mind for a better life.

ANGELA ROBERTSHAW

Madelaine had been receiving reflexology and Reiki for some time. On Friday I mentioned that I was teaching a First Degree class the following day. That evening she called to say she would like to attend.

Next day she said how surprised she was to be there, but that it was very important as it was something for herself. Although she had suffered several bereavements and a lot of stress in the previous 12 months, she was the life and soul of the group. Recently I talked to her about her Reiki experiences. She has used it on herself mainly – she has suffered further bereavement and anxiety but said that Reiki helps her to cope and she Reikies herself to sleep. She remembers the experience of the attunement sometimes – the room, the sensations, the breath, and the peace she felt. Her life problems continue but she has found great support in her Reiki.

Val had a successful operation for cancer of the oesophagus but the lymph in her throat was leaking badly. Two further operations failed to halt this. When her relative, Sheelagh, called me, Val was under sedation but still restless, in intensive care. Her immediate family went to say their farewells – it had all seemed so sudden. I told Sheelagh, who has First Degree Reiki, to ask permission to go to see her, and to simply hold her hand. She also obtained permission from the family for full distant healing. This was on the Wednesday. Sheelagh began on the Wednesday afternoon, I began sending on the Wednesday evening. We continued on the next day and I asked another person to send as well.

The feedback was truly amazing.

By the Thursday a.m., Val's blood pressure had altered, she was not losing the fluids at the same rate as previously, and though still sedated was peaceful and calm. By the Friday she had improved to such an extent that the doctors were talking of the possibility of a further operation. The family's response was that as she had improved so much in the first 48 hours, they did not wish her to have another operation at that point. She has never had another operation.

Val's progress has continued. We sent more Reiki when the wounds where the tubes entered the body became infected.

She has been at home now for a long time. She is eating normal foods, talking and walking. The family have sent their grateful thanks for all the love and help. I look forward to a time when maybe they may choose to learn Reiki for themselves.

I taught my mother Reiki when she was 76. At 77 I taught her Second Degree. She has never read a book about it, doesn't know what 'New Age' is and has the most direct and simple trust in it of anyone I have taught. She practises her Second Degree daily. I send her lists of people, make special requests for extra help when someone is very ill, or needs urgent help. Mother is almost completely deaf in both ears, and is slowly losing her sight as a result of macular degeneration; and yet, through Reiki, she has a new job, a new role for the rest of her life.

After many years of total commitment and hard work, a young friend of mine, Ben, is on the verge of success with an album coming out shortly. Four weeks ago he rang and asked me to send some Second Degree to his career. He was feeling nervous and confused, not able to believe that he was finally nearing his life-long goal. I sent to his life and career. When I spoke to him three weeks later, he told me everything was going unbelievably well, with glowing reviews in the musical papers, a live interview on the radio and a series of gigs. He was feeling more relaxed and confident. In his weekend job as a waiter at a club he also received promotion to head waiter and kitchen manager. As he laughingly said, this wasn't exactly what he had in mind when he called! He is fascinated by Reiki and is planning to learn it in the near future.

ANGI ON BECOMING A MASTER

Its simplicity is immediately recognizable. Its power and profundity take the rest of your life to comprehend.

For me, becoming a Master was the beginning of understanding how much I don't know, and how much more I have to trust in Reiki. The hardest thing is to look for the light always, even when all you can see is darkness.

MIDGE

Midge had a bone marrow transplant in March and was very ill with a kidney infection. He has improved amazingly and the transplant has taken. Midge had two Reiki treatments soon after the operation and was out flying his powerkite and playing tennis long before he had been expected to feel any recovery.

Midge writes, 'Reiki to me is a complete form of body revitalization. I feel that an individual will get out of it what he or she is mentally prepared to put in and work with; having an open mind and not presenting any mental doubts or barriers helps the Reiki do its job.

'I personally am still very new and fresh to this form of treatment and am looking to get out of it an inner calm and more relaxed disposition. I find that it eases my stresses and helps me find a more peaceful state of mind. During Reiki I find I can relax and let my mind drift into a more transient, sleepy state of consciousness as I relax. The extremities of my body become cold. When the Reiki is concentrated on a particular part of my body I sometimes find that I feel a warm sensation in the muscles surrounding this particular area. After about an hour of Reiki I feel quite tired and maybe a little drained. This seems to last for the rest of the day. It's not until some time later, usually the next day after a good sleep, that I feel the benefit – who knows how my body feels so fresh and reenergized when it has recovered. It is as if the Reiki has flushed out my system and given me an extra boost. I'm sure it works for the individual in different ways but for me I feel it offers relaxation and revitalization.'

CATH M

I began having Reiki treatments about a year after my mother died as I felt I was falling apart. I felt detached from my body and was carrying the responsibility of all the other members of my family. Reiki gave me a turnaround. It showed me I must only worry about myself. I had the first treatment in June which made a shift that continued from one treatment to the next. In September my mother-in-law became unwell. During the next treatment I decided I would like to learn Reiki for myself. In October she was diagnosed with cancer. Learning became imperative so I enquired at the local technical college. The information came but I didn't feel at all comfortable for some reason, but I desperately wanted to help myself and my husband deal with our grief and mother-in-law with her pain. I knew there was not much time. My therapist called and said, 'You must learn with Sandi, she will teach you what you need to know'. I called Sandi who had a class in our area some months ahead but one further away that very weekend. I was working nights as a nurse at the time and knew I was on duty at the weekend, also we run a hill farm of two thousand sheep, but I booked anyway! I managed to change my duty with a colleague, and my husband, Steve, drove me to the class which was over three hours' drive from us – and then returned to the farm. Added to the chaos, my mother-in-law was due home to live with us on the Friday. I felt I was abandoning her but a voice in me said, 'How much of a commitment can you make to this?'

The class was magic. It was all I had hoped for and more. The Reiki was such a comfort to my mother-in-law, even though she would only let me hold her feet. I gave her regular treatments which she found very comforting. Her cold legs warmed up. She seemed to cope with the cancer very well. We could all see a difference in her. As I treated her in bed one day it felt as if her head had opened up with light. My hands felt as if they were hovering.

After she died I gave the Reiki attention to Steve who was very responsive. He said it was like a time warp. He doesn't get much time off, being a farmer, and during the Reiki treatment he would drift away. At the end of what could have been an hour he said it only felt like five minutes. He coped very well.

I went on to learn Second Degree and held some classes at the farm which was wonderful. Each time there was a class something would change. During one I decided to knock the two small rooms into one and create a view of the valley. Gradually the light is coming into our lives more as we continue to put in more windows and paint more walls. We have also since had a baby girl who is another source of light. Second Degree gives me reassurance with situations I have no control over, like when my young son drives up the mountain in the dark at night to rescue a sick cow! I feel I can protect my family by just being at home and sending them Reiki. It's the best I can do and I leave it at that.

I have used Reiki on my patients. One lady was in a permanent vegetative state but could hear and responded with body language when she was not comfortable. Reiki calmed her down and I felt it must have been such a comfort to her to receive some form of communication that she could understand with her feelings. It felt very powerful in a powerless situation. I also used to help a man with terminal illness. I used to calm his pain just by holding his feet. He loved it.

I have used Reiki with the farm animals on many occasions. One cow was very nervous and agitated during calving examination. I gave her Reiki to her head, neck and lower spine and she noticeably calmed down.

SANDI

Insight

Animals have no mind to get in the way when healing is offered to them. They are naturally open and responsive. Animals sense when help is at hand and even cross their usual boundaries in order to seek you out.

I was visiting Cath and Steve's farm to teach a class. I am always greeted by the 11 farm dogs who guard it well, but not being a great lover of dogs they seemed very scary en masse, like a pack of hungry wolves. The leader of the pack was called Jack. He was top dog and let me know it. Steve would tie him up when I came! This time Jack was marginally less fierce as he had damaged his back leg falling off the quad bike and couldn't put it down. The Reiki class went well.

The second day as we were having lunch, Jack came through the kitchen door. Being farm dogs, none of them are allowed indoors. Cath was very surprised but knew something was wrong with him. I was even more surprised when he came straight to me, lay down and held the damaged leg up towards me. It was very tense and swollen. I put my hands round his paw but not directly on it. It was burning with heat. I was careful not to look him in the eye as I still feared for the loss of my nose! After about ten minutes the heat began to subside, his leg extended and relaxed towards me. He gave a sigh. The swelling had noticeably gone down. Suddenly he looked up, retrieved his leg and went off out to the yard. Apparently he went back out with the pack that day to round up some sheep. He had got better and in the process given me renewed faith in dogs. He was my buddy. Unfortunately he was run over the next year.

SUSIE

Jennifer and Irene lived in Italy and, as was custom there in the autumn, had picked wild mushrooms in the hills. After supper they both became very sick. It was three days before they were eventually taken to hospital with kidney failure. Things got worse as all their organs went into shock and began to fail. Jennifer's sister-in-law Susie, had learnt Second Degree Reiki with me some years before and she called and asked if I could send some to them. I set the phone tree in motion to get a group of students to co-ordinate a treatment for nine o'clock that night. As we sent the Reiki we both felt a coldness. Then a sudden wave or rush happened and we felt as if a switch had gone on or a tap had been opened. I saw a white dove float up out of Jennifer, and felt happy. Some weeks later when they were back at home it transpired that Jennifer had felt a sudden wave of energy turn around in her and at that moment she had known she would be all right. It was at nine o'clock on the night we sent Reiki.

NANCY

My mother and father were returning from Washington. Dad had been away for nearly a year. I had arranged for a taxi to pick them up at the airport and bring them the 70 miles home. The taxi driver called me on the phone as he couldn't find them anywhere. The plane had landed and he had been looking for them for over an hour and a half. I told him it would be all right. I sat down and sent Second Degree Reiki to the situation. One minute after finishing the phone rang. It was Mum, they had been found.

I have just taken some exams at school. I used Second Degree every day for each exam and really felt I could do anything. It made me feel in control and gave me peace of mind that I could do something to help myself.

SUSIE

We went to Tasmania in 1993 for a family holiday. As our 13-year-old son was desperate to bungee jump neither of us said no but were very apprehensive about the dangers; we were really unhappy about it. I sent Reiki to the situation. As it happened, after the jump before my son, the bungee crane broke down without explanation and could not be repaired!

Whenever I give Reiki to my horses they seem to yawn, lean on me, sigh and lick my feet! I presume this is a sign of enjoyment.

FRANCO

When I am nervous, say, I am giving a presentation, I get physical symptoms such as pains in the stomach. I place my hands there until the feeling in my body eases and find the nervousness in my head has gone also. I use the Reiki when I am really tired from long-distance travelling. It recovers my strength and energy.

SHARON

Since taking Masters Level 1 I have noticed how much hotter my hands have become during hands-on treatments, especially on myself. I immediately go very deep, straight down, as if sucked in to a beautiful place. It is very intense. I feel quite spaced out until I do the finishing-off technique.

In 1994 my Grandad was very ill after suffering a stroke. He was taken to hospital with kidney failure. As I was unable to visit him, I gave him Second Degree Reiki every night at about the same time. Two days before I was due to visit him the doctors said he was really bad and would only last a few days. When I sent the Reiki he always seemed peaceful. One night as I sent it to him I felt myself beside his bed holding his hand, stroking him and saying, 'It's OK Grandad, you can let go, there's nothing to be frightened of'. I looked towards the end of his bed where a fantastic bright light had appeared. It startled me but was not frightening. I looked at Grandad and he looked at me. I took his hand into part of the light, out of the light a hand came to meet his. I turned to look at him in the bed but it was not like my old Grandad, he looked so young. When I completed the Reiki I felt intense emotions and began to cry. I pulled myself together by making myself a cup of tea. As the kettle boiled my sister rang from the hospital to say that Grandad had just died. She and Mum had left him for that moment, but when they went back in the cubicle they both said how he seemed to look like a young man. At first I had thought it was my imagination but the evidence was such a comfort to me. I told Grandma what I had seen. She cried but said it was also a comfort to her.

My mother was involved in a serious car crash where a man fell asleep at the wheel on the motorway and pushed her car over a five-metre precipice. It had rolled down the steep embankment. She had a broken jaw, broken ribs, collapsed lung, and a severe break in the brachial plexus in her shoulder. This left her paralysed in her right arm and in agonizing pain. She spent a lot of time in intensive care and physiotherapy. I sent her Reiki every day. I always seemed to pick up her pain in my arm. Sometimes it hurt so much it would make me cry but I felt it doing her good. Sometimes I would send it to the whole of her or just her arm. Always I would feel the intensity of her pain. She was taking a strong painkiller every four hours but still I could feel it. Her arm is now a lot better and I still send her regular treatments. I instantly know when she has been overdoing things, I can feel it in my body, but the feelings always go away when I give thanks. I find it useful as I then know there is a particular problem and will keep my hands still until the pain or heat subsides. This regularly happens to me when I am giving hands-on treatments to my clients. I know it is not my pain, and I know it will go away.

My nephew was knocked down by a car outside his school and badly grazed his back. As I gave him Reiki at a distance my whole head filled with gorgeous light. I felt it was him – his spirit – it was not my light. It enveloped me. It then dropped away. It felt as if a piece of lost, floating spirit that separated from his body during the shock had integrated with mine for safety. The Reiki offered it back within his body and he recovered remarkably well without being too scared by the experience.

My sister-in-law was in pain with a knee problem and was being sent to a specialist by the doctor. I gave her some hands-on Reiki for about 15 minutes after which the pain lifted and she has never had it since.

GLENYS

It is over 20 years since I had my bowel removed due to acute ulcerative colitis. I have managed really well but also suffered greatly. Unfortunately it seems as if my daughter has inherited the disease. When I took Reiki 2 she was the first person to send the Reiki to. I have her in my box of names which I give to every night. I saw her recently and she said she hasn't had a sign of it for the last four months.

I can always feel the Reiki, it seems to switch on in my hand by just thinking about it. If I see someone in need or a hurt animal my hands begin to tingle and become extremely hot. I am almost compelled by the need to act.

Since the day I first came to Reiki I haven't smoked a cigarette or eaten meat. It was not a conscious thing, it just happened. My intuition and conscience seem to have awoken. My sense of right and wrong have magnified. How I came to Reiki I don't really know. I just heard it somewhere and while out shopping one day I asked in a little book shop in the arcade if they had any books on the subject. The lad there was new and couldn't find anything on the shelves. He looked in the back and found a copy of *Reiki – a beginner's guide* by Sandi Leir-Shuffrey.

I bought it and read it straight through, fascinated and at once familiar. I called the number in the back and spoke to Sandi. The book was not supposed to have been sold for at least another six weeks as it was before publishing date, but I had found it. Sandi happened to live only an hour away from me and had a class the next month. I went for a treatment and immediately began to open up spiritually. The rest is history.

Before Reiki I was trapped in a bubble, bouncing around and hitting the sides but now I feel spiritually free. On the outside, my circumstances seem to have got more painful, but inside I have become me again.

PENNY

I do Reiki on myself, mostly, last thing at night. As soon as I put my hands on myself they become extremely hot and fizzy, like hot velvet. I can see areas of shifting colour, a bit like a lava lamp! Colours moving, shifting, often magenta or purple to shades of blue, ochre, grey and turquoise. I feel as if I am plugged into a major power source. Life force rushes through me from the top of my head to my feet, out through the room and across the common! It is like a search light pouring through and around me. There is an underlying low-level vibration, a slow throbbing throughout. It feels as if I disintegrate, lose form, and become fabulous liquid, become light and colour. Then I reform with crisper edges. I feel more positive and safe. Sometimes I fall into a comatose sleep and wake up refreshed in the morning.

Once my friend was treating her son in the same room as I was, I could see blue sparks of light coming out of her hands and off the ends of her fingers. He seemed to find it very relaxing and energizing.

I often treat my horse. She twitches all over as if there were flies landing on her; I think it must be the blue light sparks landing. She sometimes leans into me and sighs, accepting everything, but sometimes she doesn't want to know and walks away. She decides, she will even nudge my hands off when she is ready. Last year she tore a ligament in her hind leg which needed long rest. She accepted everything she could get, then. My hands would burn with heat but it seemed to ease her pain and stiffness. She is very sensitive and responsive.

SARAH C

On the second day of my course my Reiki partner, Jill, felt my leg bone 'almost move' just below the right knee. Unbeknown to her I had severely broken this knee in 1993. Since my accident, although I had regained most of the movement I had not been able to squat down fully. When I went home after the Reiki, as my leg felt so flexible, I decided to squat down and yes, I could! The amazing thing was, I could even get back up again afterwards. I didn't tell anyone for three days, I just kept checking I could still do it and I still can!

As I gave Reiki to my best friend one day, spots of light appeared as soon as I put my hands on her. They seemed to be in the corner of the room. My immediate thought was that the angels had arrived. The hairs on my arms stuck straight out during the whole treatment. My friend's face was very red. She also saw the angels arrive and felt as though a big ball of lovely warm swirling light was by her face. I then saw an image of a young girl aged about six or seven playing on a swing – it was obviously her favourite place and she had lovely long hair. I knew at once this was my friend's sister who had died from cancer at the age of seven, a year before my friend was born. I had never seen a picture of her.

My friend saw the same image and apparently when the sister lost her hair from treatment, her mum bought her a wig which she loved! Needless to say, my friend now wants to learn Reiki.

CHARLES

I was recently visiting Miami with time to spare for sight-seeing. I booked a taxi for three hours to take me round 'the good, the bad and the ugly' parts of town. I used Reiki to protect myself on this journey as some areas were quite dangerous. I walked through the Haiti Quarter by myself, through the Voodoo shops and the bars. I felt safe.

I am often called upon to give lectures, talks and attend conferences with my work in different parts of the world. I once gave a talk in Adelaide, Australia, that had to be exactly 45 minutes long. Firstly I gave myself some hands on Reiki to re-energize myself after the long flight. I then sent Reiki to the talk. It seems to enable a flow, a rhythm to take place. The talk finished in 44 minutes and 59 seconds! It was very successful. Reiki seems to help envelop each segment of the talk, and the talk as a whole, including the audience. It seems as if I am enveloping each piece and all things simultaneously and making them mine.

After taking the Master's Level 1 things seem to activate more immediately and the results seem to show remarkably quickly. I can see how easy it would be for Reiki to be abused in the sense that it could be just a quick fix.

As I constantly travel long distances I routinely use Reiki as a form of protection to my journey. I go through a process of envelopment of the object – the plane, the journey, the engine, the pilot, every molecule of every part of the engine and pilot, the wings, the back, the tail, the passengers. The molecules seem to fizz then fuse together into one thing. It's like protective light realms buzzing round the whole totality. It is a protection from the influence of surroundings. Things seem to light up when you think of them.

Once I was being disturbed by a very fidgety boy in the seat in front of me. We had a long way to go, so I used Reiki. He immediately fell asleep and woke up when we were within half an hour of landing.

ANGELA ROBERTSHAW

For me Reiki is like jumping into the light – like learning to swim and finally having the courage to make the leap from the pool's edge to the lovely clear blue water that you've always wanted to jump into!

It's as good as you always knew it would be, but the only thing that stopped you was fear.

Anger will anaesthetize. Be careful not to fall asleep again.

10 THINGS TO REMEMBER

1 *Reiki is gentle and uncomplicated.*

2 *It increases confidence and gives a greater connection to the world.*

3 *Reiki is easy. It enables you to give something back.*

4 *The Stillpoint School of Reiki is in direct lineage from Dr Usui.*

5 *Reiki fills in the missing piece of the puzzle.*

6 *Happiness is a common side effect of treatment.*

7 *Reiki gives confidence and courage to face all fears.*

8 *Reiki fills the emptiness with the feeling of bliss.*

9 *People find it easier to give up bad habits and addictions with self-treatment.*

10 *Reiki sounds too good to be true, but the common experience is that it is true.*

14

The nature of consciousness

In this chapter you will learn:
- *about pure consciousness, beyond the personality, that is the ultimate goal of a human being*
- *how Reiki can help you, in a simple way, to return to joy.*

Wisdom is the greatest cleanser.

Swami Sri Yukteswarji

The Master's gift is to allow change to take place in the level of consciousness, but this must first be familiar to them if the energy of the teacher can reach that of the student and influence them into awakening.

Insight
Only a lamp that is lit can light the lamps that are not yet lit.

Shri Hans Ji Maharaj

Consciousness is not the opposite of unconsciousness. Consciousness is Being. It is impersonal. It resides at the sublime level of existence of the body. It is at the heart of the Universe. It is an oscillating rhythm that has no individuality, no personality yet it has the supreme intelligence to travel anywhere and manifest as anything simultaneously.

We all have the privilege to be a witness to this Grace and to be able to be supported by it constantly even when we are unaware of it. The Creator has said, 'Even when you deny me, I am with you.'

The complete unity of consciousness cannot be divided, or separated, not even in experience. When I dip into that place of stillness within by placing my hands on my physical body to ease the discomfort, settle the particles, hold still the mind, I may then reach an experience that is consciousness united itself. It is unlike any other experience. It creates unity in the consciousness of the whole, not just the one. It is a constant underlying force that does not need to rise to the surface of our mind and intellect to be understood but it needs for us to leave the realm of illusory surface, mind, body, emotion, soul, by releasing them like helium balloons and once more to take up our rightful throne on the seat of all knowledge, the place where the spark of creative intelligence is awakened into being. From this place we can expand our restrictions and limited viewpoints, belief systems and body in its dis-ease to create anew.

The feeling of surrender to pure consciousness is a tasty carrot that creates dissatisfaction on returning to the solid surface view. Once we have seen our true nature we flail around like drowning swans, until we decide to focus on being rather than doing. Life has to go on and we must still be responsible for our commitments in the world, our family, our job, our friends. But no man should be denied his right to know the presence of his creator through direct experience.

It takes many different approaches to teach people about consciousness as there is a diversity of people, all unique in their struggle or journey to find purpose and meaning in life. Levels are attained and become spontaneous as we awaken.

Different states of consciousness are available to us – sleeping, dreaming, wakefulness, transcendence, cosmic consciousness, God consciousness and Unity consciousness. Most of us live in the first three and are happy with that but once the fourth, transcendence, is experienced, a doorway opens to the other realms. There is no going back. Reiki practice enables us to slip into the transcendent state and become so familiar with it that it begins to remain during wakefulness. This is why, once you learn Reiki, the world will never look the same again.

There is a Zen question: 'What is your true face? What was your true nature before your parents were born?' Are you not yet aware that you existed then also? Can you get a glimpse of having been here all along?

In reaching out the hands to touch we cannot help but experience touching. The receiver cannot help but experience being touched. In this connection, awareness of other is an underlying presence. Yet through the process and intent of sincerity, compassion and truth, the Being is felt beyond the sensation of touching. Hence, when we receive a treatment we dive inwards away from the surface experience of touch and being touched into an unfamiliar terrain of expanded awareness. It is unfamiliar only because we rarely allow ourselves the time, focus or stillness to see it, yet it is definitely not something new. There always remains the sensation of, 'Ah yes, you again, thank you'.

The more we dive in the more we want. For those of us addicted to substances, emotions and behaviour in the manifest world, this is guaranteed to be the safest direction in which to place our addiction. Become addicted to bliss and you will be free. Regularly reminding ourselves where bliss resides and what it can do, brings about a recognition of priority. So few people have Divine Being as their priority, they find the very term embarrassing. Andrew Cohen says: 'People give more attention to sex than to God.'

Why are we so afraid of God? Is it because when we admit we believe but don't really know that our fear and sadness will be exposed? Why will people do anything to be well but not cross the barrier of what others might think of them? Why will they not admit that a simple system of hands-on healing could change their life and at last put them in touch with renewed energy and freedom? On your death bed will you still care what the neighbours think? Just contemplate, for a moment, the absurdity of our mind. If you were to be reborn at this moment what would you do differently? How would you want to be?

It becomes imperative to disallow negative mind talk if you are to know your true self. Your mind is not you, it is just your mind – chaos in motion. When we wake up tired and low, the mind is quick to jump in and say, 'Oh God …' (that's a good start) '… I am feeling so depressed. Everything is going wrong, I haven't enough money, my relationships don't work, I am a hopeless parent.' STOP! Do not allow it to continue.

The body may feel heavy, the head full of the fog of unfulfilled dreams and the posture slumped with the imploding energy. Be quick to catch yourself before naming the state and say, 'No! I will not have unhappiness/depression/pain in my life.' As you naturally place your hands on your head in despair to say 'Oh no!', put them there instead with kindness and compassion. Refuse to listen to what the mind has to say. Hold it still with the hands, allow the thoughts to come and go without entertaining them, let them settle down, let them quieten. Whatever you allow in your head will create a corresponding chemical change in the body, so 'catch it quick' and allow change to take place. Practise Re-Lax Breath (see page 6) and 15 minutes of self-treatment to head and heart positions. Affirm 'Just for today my mind is at rest' and 'Just for today I am in a state of forgiveness'.

Practise the finishing-off technique to awaken the physiology and encourage the energy to flow. Practise some good stretching to expand the arms at the shoulders, the head, the waist and the ankles. Every time the mind falls in again in its monotonous drone beginning 'Oh no!', disallow it to continue. Keep the spine supple and strong.

'Just for today I am at peace.' Spend some time in light, air and nature. Breathe a full breath. Congratulate yourself at the end of the day but never forget to give thanks to that life force for holding you up so you can experience all these things.

If life were a river where would you be? Drowning, lost in
the rapids, stuck in the stagnant eddy, in a boat with one oar,
or a boat with no oars at all, climbing out on the bank or
swimming about having a great time with your friends?
First learn to swim then, if you were to fall into a river, you
would have a good chance of being able to rescue yourself
and swim to safety. You may also be given the chance to
rescue someone else.

Nothing is static. Everything is constantly changing. Nothing can
remain unchanged except the nothingness itself. Yet that too is in
motion and constantly becoming. To begin with it is enough to
address the opposite quality to our perpetual negative patterns.
Yet this inevitably leaves the balance unstable. Ultimately, to balance
any extreme it is only important to focus on the midway, the centre
of the scale, the unmanifest. Through self-treatment, focus and
intent the midway becomes a still and secure reference point.
The word secure conjures up not only stability but also non-change.
In the place of stillness, tranquillity and serenity, the opposites
unite and become mere possibilities of choice. Whichever way
we choose to act will create our pathway. Neither way is right or
wrong, although one may be more beneficial than the other.

Resting in the centre brings about clarity of mind and clarity of
judgement. Consciousness does not mind which choice we make
at any given moment as it will support us whatever our decisions.
Through the power of Reiki and its quality of love anything can be
achieved. It takes our effort to maintain the connection by constant
self-referral through practice.

Why is it so hard to be a human being? Is it because we constantly
try to become rather than be?

Just as we take medicine or apply a bandage to a wound,
meditation on being via the body, mind, emotion and soul will
heal them all. Beginning with the soul. The body is the slower,
denser vibration that may take longer to repair. Over seven years

every single cell in the human body is replaced, so it may take seven years for the body to repair its structure and its memory completely.

Insight

If life has become mundane, tiring and routine, then you have closed the door to the experience of an extraordinary magic. In order for healing to take place you must start to imagine and begin to dream. Miracles happen when your fear has burnt away, the smoke screen has cleared and the faith in yourself returns.

To create well-being where illness reigns takes effort, commitment, determination and trust. Reiki is the starting point for change to take place. The body can become well, the emotions can become calm and the mind can become clear. Vitality returns with a sense of peace, happiness and enjoyment of life. Only through a change in consciousness can the repair to the damage from the past become permanent. Treatment and self-treatment become daily practice to retain the new-found state of balance. Spiritual understanding gradually creeps into every moment, every breath.

As we grow in understanding and awareness we begin to sense that a part of us is merely witnessing the physical and mental planes. It is as if we are simultaneously a part of our life yet detached from it. Happiness comes about as a state of being once the witness and the witnessed integrate. It is my experience that the witness comes forward to inhabit the life, personality and even the body, at the same time as the awareness begins to step back from its attachment to the chaotic mind and emotional state. There comes a time when a shift has taken place that cannot be undone. The vision of the world is from a different point of view and consequently the world becomes a different world.

Regular Reiki self-treatment will bring about the integration. It may take one session but it may take 20 or 30 years! When the shift takes place the Chakras come into a new alignment.

From the time of the first initiation of First Degree the source of life is directly accessible to you. From learning and practising with the Second Degree symbols and mantras, a depth of understanding and lateral vision unfolds. From the undertaking of and commitment to the Master's symbol and mantra at Master's Level 1, the light begins to burn from within the heart, purifying thought, emotion and healing all past grief, anger and fear. The Inner Child grows up and becomes you. From the act of being a dedicated and committed teaching Master the gratitude and humility grow as the gift begins to spread itself, producing unbounded, quiet joy. What a magnificent process. It is time to wake up to feel what it is to be truly human again, to feel the way you always knew you could, to be the person you have always known you were. I honour the sacredness of this gift and offer it to you.

> *Beingness can act in the world only with the aid of the body.*
>
> Sri Nisargadatta Maharaj

Insight

In order to make changes in health and happiness permanent, it is necessary to apply discipline in daily practice. Practice the piano for an hour a day and in eight years you could be a concert pianist! Practice Reiki self-treatment for an hour a day and in eight years who knows, you could be enlightened!

Questions and answers

Q *It scares me, all this colours and lights and hearing voices, it sounds like madness. Should I learn?*

A You only get what you can handle with Reiki. If you are afraid of this it probably won't occur. When you see colours in a deep state of relaxation it can be joyous not scary. Have confidence in yourself and always practise the finishing-off technique and give thanks.

Q *You say not to treat the mentally ill. I have acute anxiety with phobias and am not very balanced but would like to be healed. I am taking Prozac but feel really weird on it and am not happy about taking drugs. What can I do?*

A Treatment can be very effective in calming the mind and the emotions and balancing the chemistry, especially adrenalin and seratonin. As long as the practitioner is fully aware of your condition and you let them know as soon as you feel unwell or ungrounded then it should be of great benefit to you. Have a treatment first to see how sensitive you are to it and gradually progress to learning when you feel more balanced. Ultimately, self-treatment would be good for you to be able to do to control your hormones and chemistry. Once you have learnt Reiki it may be possible to reduce the Prozac gradually but only under the supervision of your doctor. You must never stop suddenly as it produces serious withdrawal symptoms. Reiki can help these symptoms and maintain your balance once free of drugs.

Q *I feel overwhelmed now that I have Reiki 1 as everywhere I go I see people in need and suffering, I feel I can't do enough. I am getting very emotional. Am I doing things right?*

A Do not feel responsible for everyone else on the planet and their pain. The best you can do is to keep yourself in order with self-treatment. Lend a hand to help your immediate friends and family. Others will be led to healing through their suffering in the end. We cannot make it all right for everyone but make it all right in your own life.

Q *I am a Spiritual Healer and have learnt to heal with my hands in the Aura. Do I have to put hands on for Reiki to come through?*

A Reiki will come through from the Aura but it is important for the receiver to experience being held non-invasively as the healing takes place. It creates less mystery yet still addresses the spirit. Reiki form is about holding the spirit within the body, not contacting spirit in spite of the body.

Q *I am pregnant. Is there any reason why I shouldn't have Reiki?*

A It is best to leave learning until later on. Having a baby is a precious initiation in itself and is a full-time job. Receiving treatment is perfectly safe at all stages. If you have Reiki already then your hands will automatically be on the baby just beaming it love.

10 THINGS TO REMEMBER

1 *Reiki awakens the creative intelligence with which you were born.*

2 *Reiki activates the seven levels of consciousness.*

3 *Reiki allows us to touch and therefore be touched.*

4 *Reiki makes the unfamiliar familiar.*

5 *Keep thoughts active and change your mind.*

6 *Keep the body fit and supple and feed it with quality.*

7 *Spend time in nature and look at the sky.*

8 *Spend time each day in Reiki meditation, being held still in a quiet place within.*

9 *Happiness returns as a state of being.*

10 *Don't put off learning for another moment. Take Reiki into your life and it will really show you what you can do.*

Taking it further

Further reading

TRADITIONAL USUI SHIKI RYOHO REIKI

Baginski, B and Sharamon, S, *Reiki – Universal Life Energy*, Life Rhythm.

Barnett, Libby and Chambers, Maggie, *Reiki – Energy Medicine*, Healing Arts Press.

Charlish, Anne and Robertshaw, Angela, *Secrets of Reiki*, Dorling Kindersley.

Haberly, Helen, *Hawayo Takata's Story*, Archidigm.

Horan, Paula, *Empowerment through Reiki*, Lotus Light.

Leir-Shuffrey, Sandi, *Reiki – A Beginner's Guide*, Hodder & Stoughton.

Leir-Shuffrey, Sandi, *Live Better – Reiki*, Duncan Baird.

Lubeck, Walter, *Reiki: Way of the Heart*, Lotus Light.

Quest, Penelope, *Reiki*, Piatkus.

OTHER USEFUL TITLES

Bovey, Shelley, *The Empty Nest*, Pandora.

Carlson, Richard and Shield, Banjamin (eds), *Healers on Healing*, Rider.

Chopra, Deepak, *The Seven Spiritual Laws of Success*, Bantam Press.

Chopra, Deepak, *The Seven Spiritual Laws of Success for Parents*, Rider.

Chopra, Deepak, *Quantum Healing*, Bantam.

Gibran, Khalil, *The Prophet*, William Heinemann Ltd.

Golman, Daniel, *Emotional Intelligence*, Bloomsbury.

Jeffers, Susan, *Feel The Fear and Do It Anyway*, Fawcett Columbine.

Johnson, Charles, *The Yoga Sutras of Patanjali*, Watkins.

Khema, Ayya, *Being Nobody Going Nowhere – Meditations on the Buddhist Path*, Wisdom.

Long, Barry, *Ridding Yourself of Unhappiness*, The Barry Long Foundation.

Long, Barry, *The Origins of Man and the Universe*, Barry Long Books.

Mulford, Prentice, *Thought Forces*, Standard Publications.

Myss, Caroline, *Anatomy of the Spirit*, Bantam.

Myss, Caroline, *Why People Don't Heal and How They Can*, Bantam.

Ozaniec, Naomi, *Chakras for Beginners*, Hodder & Stoughton.

Parry, Robert, *Find Peace with Tai Chi*, Hodder Education.

Rael, Joseph, *Being and Vibration*, Council Oak Books.

Twan, Wanja, *In the Light of a Distant Star*, Morning Star Productions.

Wattles, Wallace and Powell, Dr Judith, *The Science of Getting Rich*, Top of the Mountain Publishing.

Wilde, Stuart, *Whispering Winds of Change*, White Dove International.

The following books contain information on affirmations:
Hay, Louise, *You Can Heal Your Life*, Eden Grove Editions.

Scheffer, Mechthild, *Bach Flower Therapy – Theory and Practice*, Thorsons.

Wilde, Stuart, *Affirmations*, White Dove International.

Information about Maharaji: Visions International, PO Box 4918, Thousand Oaks, CA 91359–4918, USA. Call (+1) 805-496-4777. Fax: (+1) 805-495-3165. www.tprf.org

Audio, video tapes and books by Barry Long from: The Barry Long Foundation, BCM, Box 876, London WC1N 3XX, England. The Barry Long Centre (Australia), PO Box 1260, Southport, Qld 4215, Australia.

Further information

For courses in the British Isles and Europe with Reiki Master Sandi Leir-Shuffrey MFA, RMA, MUKRF, FAETC, FETcert, DipIHM, please contact her directly at the address below leaving your name, address and telephone number for information, or visit the website and send her an email.

Sandi Leir-Shuffrey
The Stillpoint School of Reiki
Mulberry Cottage
St Chloe Green
Amberley
Stroud
Gloucestershire GL5 5AP
England
Tel: (44) 01453 872575
Email: info@teachyourselfreiki.co.uk
www.teachyourselfreiki.co.uk

For a Reiki governing body in the United Kingdom, contact the Reiki Federation. This is an umbrella group to uphold training standards in the UK exclusively for Reiki practitioners and Masters of all lineages. Sandi cannot personally recommend Masters who have not trained at Stillpoint but she is a member of the UK Reiki Federation.

The UK Reiki Federation
P.O. Box 1785
Andover
SP11)WB
(44)01264 773774
Email: enquiry@reikifed.co.uk
www.reikifed.co.uk

Reiki Alliance International
P.O. Box No 41
Cataldo
Idaho 83810-1041
Tel: 208-682-3535
Fax: 208-682-4848
Email: internationaloffice@reikialliance.com
www.reikialliance.com

Reiki Alliance Europe
Postbus 75523
1070
Amsterdam
Netherlands
Tel: 31-20-6719276
Email: 1101125.466@compuserve.com
Fax: 31-20-6711736

Reiki New Zealand Inc
P.O. Box 60-226
Titirangi
Auckland
Email: reiki@ihug.co.nz

Reiki Outreach International (Crisis Line) May McFadden
P.O. Box 609
Fair Oaks
California
USA
Tel: (916) 863-1500
Fax: (916) 863-6464

International Association of Reiki Professionals
P.O. Box 104
Harrisville, NH 03450
USA
Tel: (603)881-8838

Index